James Theodore Bent

A freak of freedom

The Republic of San Marino

James Theodore Bent

A freak of freedom
The Republic of San Marino

ISBN/EAN: 9783337282738

Printed in Europe, USA, Canada, Australia, Japan

Cover: Foto ©Andreas Hilbeck / pixelio.de

More available books at **www.hansebooks.com**

A FREAK OF FREEDOM

OR

THE REPUBLIC OF SAN MARINO

BY

J. THEODORE BENT

Honorary Citizen of the same

LONDON

LONGMANS, GREEN, AND CO.

1879

PREFACE.

DURING a hurried visit to San Marino in the spring of 1877, I felt so interested with the simplicity of the inhabitants, and their attachment to their freedom, that I determined when an opportunity occurred to investigate more thoroughly the story of this liberty of fifteen centuries' standing, and to ascertain whether it was *bonâ fide*, or no.

So unreliable was the scanty authority on which I had to go, with the exception of Melchiore Delfico's work, which partakes too strongly of a eulogistic form, that I found it necessary to spend some weeks amongst the Republicans, and feel greatly obliged not only

for the kind assistance afforded me in my re-
searches by everyone whom I there met, but
also for an interesting piece of parchment,
which I received shortly after my departure,
making me a citizen of the Republic, and accompanied by a letter of thanks for the interest
I had taken in all their concerns.

The results I here place before the public,
trusting that, as San Marino appeared in the
Street of Nations at the late Paris Exhibition,
others, too, may be interested to hear something of its customs and constitutions, which
furnish us with a living representative of the
Middle Ages, whilst its history mingles us in
many of the most stirring scenes which have
occurred on Italian soil.

Accommodation there is certainly limited
and primitive, but what they lack in comforts
the Sammarinesi make up for by hospitality,
and not a little was contributed to the pleasure
of our visit to this wild mountain by the atten-

tion of our host and hostess, Signor Francesco
Casali, and his wife, whose house, next to the
Franciscan gate, is most conveniently situated
for the passing traveller.

Though not offering the sight-seer attrac-
tions such as the rest of Italy possesses, San
Marino affords plenty of natural charms of
wildness and simplicity; for whilst the views
combine some of the most fantastic peaks of the
Umbrian Mountains, the study of their private
life and customs leads one to agree with their
own favourite simile, 'Here we live and die,
like the flowers of the field.'

The few illustrations introduced herein are
from some of my own sketches taken on the
spot.

J. THEODORE BENT.

FLORENCE: *December* 25, 1878.

CONTENTS.

CHAPTER I.

SAN MARINO AS IT IS.

CHAPTER II.

LEGENDARY HISTORY OF THE FOUNDATION OF
THE REPUBLIC.

(A.D. 360.)

CHAPTER III.

CHAPTER IV.

CHAPTER V.

DIFFICULTIES WITH PAPAL LEGATES.

(A.D. 1321–1367.)

CHAPTER VI.

COMMENCEMENT OF THE GOLDEN ERA IN THE UMBRIAN MOUNTAINS.

(A.D. 1378–1458.)

CHAPTER VII.

CONTINUED PROSPERITY.

(A.D. 1463–1509.)

CHAPTER VIII.

THE STAR OF ROMAGNA BEGINS TO WANE.

(A.D. 1513–1690.)

CHAPTER IX.

THE CARDINAL ALBERONI.

(A.D. 1739.)

CHAPTER X.

NAPOLEON IN ITALY.

(A.D. 1790–1824.)

CHAPTER XIV.

INTERNAL ECONOMY.

LIST OF ILLUSTRATIONS.

VIEW FROM THE BORGO

A

FREAK OF FREEDOM.

CHAPTER I.

SAN MARINO AS IT IS.

Allor che il sole i primi raggi vibra
Dall' Oriente, e impallidir fa gli astri,
Tu vedi biancheggiar di vivo lume
L'alto Titano, ove lo stanco piede
Raccolse libertade, e s'ebbe nome
Dal suo Divin Marin.   G. PAGGETTI.

SITUATED at a distance of about twelve miles
from the Adriatic at Rimini, the volcanic rock
which forms the nucleus of the small Republic
of San Marino has overlooked a great high-
road of nations for centuries. The 'via
Emilia' of Roman days is now succeeded by
the railroad from Bologna to Brindisi; and
though the traveller on the great overland

B

route to India may frequently have seen, and may frequently have heard of this small republic, yet the phases which this mountain has passed through in history are comparatively unknown to those who pass so near, and though slightly affecting the destinies of the world around it, San Marino has shown a constancy to the motto of ' liberty,' which cannot fail to contrast favourably with all other Italian communities, which centuries ago succumbed to tyranny and oppression.

A comprehensive description of San Marino is contained in the following euphonious Italian definition, 'This Republic is a mole on the cheek of a fair lady.' Nurtured and matured in the centre of everything that was Italian, yet now that Italy is itself no more but the vast sarcophagus of its former greatness, the Republic of San Marino alone remains to us as a specimen of those constitutions which formed the mediæval greatness of Florence and Venice, an idiosyncrasy in history, which through its insignificance has baffled the storms of centuries, and through its internal administration has overcome the vices which formed the ruin of its more powerful contemporaries.

It is like an echo of ages long gone by, to the traveller who visits this wild rock, to hear men anxiously discussing the qualities of the newly imported '*podestà*;' whilst to read the decisions of the 'Council of Twelve' brings back memories of dark deeds inseparably attached to the Venetian lagunes, which centuries, like the silent waters of her own Adriatic, have long since consigned to oblivion. *TARGET FOR OGGREJJ IM*

Approached from Rimini, the three towers of San Marino form a conspicuous outline on the horizon, and rise abruptly out of a plain well stocked with vineyards, and cornfields among the most fertile in Italy. The area of the Republic being only 16 square miles, the traveller is well-nigh under the shadow of the rock which forms its centre before reaching the village of Serravalle, which on this side forms the boundary of the State, and from which a steep ascent leads to the '*Borgo*,' the centre of San Marino's commercial activity.

To accomplish this ascent carriages are
obliged to seek the assistance of some oxen,
which at once bring us face to face with one of
the most productive branches of the Republic's
commerce. For the Sammarinesi are extensive
breeders of cattle, and their oxen are much
esteemed for strength, and field labour. On a fair
day in the Borgo several hundred of these oxen,
together with innumerable herds of sheep and
pigs, are exposed for sale. This monthly fair
is indeed a busy day for the Republic, everything is life and bustle in the small village
below, whilst the Città built on the rock above
is doubly sombre, left alone in its lofty solitude
to contemplate the busy hive of bees below,
of which it is, and has been for fifteen centuries,
the centre of government, and the stronghold
of their ever-vaunted liberty.

In the Borgo are found the cellars of San
Marino's wines of considerable reputation, indeed, of which Matteo Valli, writing in the seventeenth century an account of the Republic, says,
' The wines here are so pleasing, pure, grateful,
and good that they have no cause to be jealous

of the clarets of France.' From the caverns beneath the Borgo, on the hottest day of summer, a glass of wine can be got, as cool as if from an ice-house; for built under the shelter of the rock with a northern aspect the Borgo is never exposed to the midday heat of the sun, which

WINE CART IN THE BORGO.

in winter scarcely ever penetrates it. And here too is the natural curiosity of a cavern into which in summer cold air is perpetually blowing from a crevice in the mountain side, dangerous, they say, to approach without every precaution in the way of clothing.

All the elements of a primitive and rural

centre of life are here gathered together ; two miniature ‘*piazze*,’ with arcades and shops, two churches, a small inn of no very cleanly appearance, and a theatre, the main boast of which is a magnificent drop scene representing ‘liberty’ adorned in a scarcity of apparel, the head of which is a portrait of the Duchess of Acquaviva, a benefactress of the State.[1]   In the Borgo the well-to-do merchants have some tidy little villas, preferring the more active life down here to the isolation of the ‘*città*’ above. In fact, this mercantile village is the only element in the Republic to remind the traveller that he is still living in the nineteenth century ; everything else, constitutions, buildings, and inhabitants, are the relics of the past, existing in an age which can hardly call them its contemporaries.

From the Borgo two roads lead to the ‘*città*,’ one of which is steep and rugged, and abandoned now entirely to pedestrians, for within the last two years the Republic has con-

---

[1] Vide ch. xiv.

structed a good road for carriages, which enters the town at the other side.

Approaching by the footpath the ascent is very trying; but at every step the enchanting view over the plain and the Adriatic well repays the enterprise, and when the ' *Porta alla Rupe*' is reached the traveller is loath to leave it for the dark streets within. Suffice it to say, they are long, and gloomy, and on each side lined by the so-called '*palazzi*' of the nobility, until at length a little '*piazza*' is reached, where stands a miniature fish market, quietly reposing in a hole in the wall, for the republicans never think of traffic up here, and are far too conservative to buy fish elsewhere than in the Borgo. In fact in this long street, a druggist and a tobacconist alone seem to be in request, and these are of a very second-rate type.

Ascending rapidly by a newly paved street, the '*Pianello*'—so-called from being the only level ground in the Città—is reached. This is entirely unique in itself. Surrounded on three sides by the Government offices, namely the

Council Hall, the Audience Chambers and the
Law Courts. the Post-Office and clock tower, and
one or two palaces, all of them of small merit
in the artistic line, but from their antiquity
inspiring feelings of respect, if not of admira-
tion. It was with regret I learnt that the
more energetic rulers of to-day purpose putting
a new façade on their Audience Chambers.
In short, as says Auger St. Hippolyte, 'There
exists here in truth no art, or anything which
recalls the vices of great cities, or the corruption of the smaller ones, behind the immorality
of the great.'

In the centre of this Pianello stands a
handsome statue, presented by the above-
mentioned Duchess of Acquaviva, a white
marble figure representing Liberty, whilst
underneath the whole is one vast reservoir
which provides the inhabitants with a never-
failing supply of water in the driest summer.
Against the wall of the Post-Office, the
standard of weights and measures is posted up,
for the benefit of the inhabitants, and here
everyone who expects a letter must repair at

the time of the arrival of the post, for a post-
man is not yet an established necessity in our
little State; and it is only of late years that the
post has arrived as far as this, formerly stop-
ping in the Borgo, whither expectant ' *cittadini* '
had to descend. Now when the addresses have
been carefully copied in a book, a bell is
rung, and the letters are distributed to those
present on their giving a written receipt,
whilst those who are absent have to wait for
their letters until the following day.

The fourth side of this Pianello is entirely
occupied by a most glorious view over the
fantastic Umbrian Mountains, the country of
Raphael and Perugino, where, heaped pro-
miscuously against one another, these mountains assume those grotesque forms so often
depicted by these great masters, but so seldom
realised as exact representations of nature.
Here when the sun sets may be seen nine or
ten distinct distances of the Apennines, of
which San Marino is the headland, so to speak,
rising abruptly about 2,300 feet above the
level of the sea. But let us ascend higher to

the ' *Castello*,' from whence a more perfect *coup
d'œil* of the neighbourhood may be obtained.
On ascending past the church, the shrine of the
patron saint, the ' *Rocca* ' or citadel of San
Marino is seen towering high above the rest of
the town, and standing out grandly against the
sky, a bold continuation of the grey tufous
rock on which the city is built, so similar in
colour to the natural fortifications around it,
that it is hard to define where nature ends, and
man's art begins.

A stiff climb brings the traveller to the
portal, the door of which is opened by a
custodian whose hoary locks and tottering step
correspond well with the scene around; a few
herbs and a good colony of rabbits seem to
occupy more of his attention than the spare
number of prisoners of whom he has the
charge. Close to the gate are shown two
miniature cannons, both in a state of the greatest
decrepitude and neglect, which were bought
in 1824 ' *ex senatus consulto* ' to assist on festive
occasions. The bastions and defences are all
of the most ordinary nature, and hardly merit-

ing the name, if not placed in so naturally strong a position. It has frequently been argued in illustration of San Marino's good behaviour, that the prisons are in so small request; one traveller alleges that the only prisoner he there beheld was left in charge of the gate and garden during the temporary absence of the gaoler, and on being asked why he did not take his departure also, he affirmed that his quarters were far too comfortable.

Be this as it may, the fact seems to be that only cases of short imprisonment are kept here, such for instance as occur after a brawl at any fair, and that a treaty has been entered into with Italy, by which all malefactors condemned to a long term of imprisonment in the galleys are transferred to the care of that country, and all the horrible dungeons beneath have long since been disused.

Two malefactors were enjoying a temporary detention here during my visit, one for forgery, and another for attempted assassination, prior to their transportation; ' enjoying ' I say advisedly, for the large whitewashed cells, fresh air, and lovely view would tempt even the most upright to a breach of the peace. They are exhibited to the public by means of small windows let into the cell door, through which they can put their heads, and wish the visitor good-day.

On ascending the tower, the bell is shown which calls the inhabitants to the general '*arringo*' or public council, and is only rung on this or some other equally urgent occasion. But by far the greatest reward for the tedious ascent is the glorious view, which here comprises ridge over ridge of the Apennines into the dimmest distance on the one side, whilst on the other extends the plain of Rimini, and the distant Adriatic which waters it ; beyond this, on a clear morning at sunrise, the distant peaks of the Dalmatian mountains appear like a narrow girdle on the horizon, whilst the waters of the Adriatic sparkle with the sails of gaudy fishing smacks lit up by the morning sun.

No better point than this can be taken for viewing the surrounding country. In mid distance on the side of the Apennines rises San Marino's twin sister fortress San Leo, where the saintly companion of the founder of the Republic established his rival, but not so durable, community. The mountains of Carpegna form a background on the left, overlooking the cradle of the Montefeltrian family; below, the river, called after the Republic, forms the natural boundary of San Marino's restricted territory. The great stone bed of the Marrechia carries the eye down to the coast on the north, the bed of a winter torrent, which washes the base of *Verruchio*, a stronghold of the Malatesti, the scene of many a tragedy enacted by that blood-thirsty race, where Giovanni the Lame slew the erring Paolo and Francesca da Rimini, as sung by Dante in his 'Inferno.' The small hamlets belonging to the Republic lie scattered beneath, Factano, Mongiardino and the thrifty Borgo ; whilst in the far distance the eye rests on the towers of Cesena, and Pesaro, and, if the air be clear, on Ravenna and the lowlands of the Comachio. Here imagination may trace the little Rubicon now hardly discernible in its marshy bed.

In the dialect of the country this castle is

called Monte Guaita, from a word *guaitare*,
signifying to watch. Two other towers occupy
two separate heights, rejoicing in the names of
Monte Cucco, and Monte Gista ; but they are
towers merely for ornament, and built to keep
up the idea of the three '*pennæ*' of San Marino,
which are everywhere depicted, emblazoned on
their money, coats of arms, and flag, and
printed on their stamps, and inseparably
connected with their motto of 'liberty.' This
word unconsciously takes us back to the
ancient Celtic derivative '*Penn*' signifying
something ending in a point. The Alpes
Penninæ are now represented by the Apennines, whilst near San Marino the names of
Penna Billi, and Penna Rossa, show the same
origin as our Ben Nevis and Penmanmaur. But
nowhere is the feathery termination of a mountain peak more justly appropriate than at San
Marino, as the inhabitants apparently recognize
by surmounting each tower in their coat of arms
with a feather.

During the inclemency of a Sammarinese
winter these steep streets are covered with

frost and snow, and the inhabitants take advantage of the season to indulge themselves in a species of Canadian ' Toboggning,' which is here called the ' *liscia*.' Down the centre of the main street of the Città the snow is swept off two furrows, which then freeze hard ; and down these small sledges are propelled with surprising velocity, and, guiding his sledge by a piece of wood attached, the adventurous republican is generally accompanied in his wild career by a female seated on his knee.

In February 1740, Enrico Enriquez, writing from San Marino,[1] thus graphically describes the effect of such atmospheric severity on an inhabitant of the more genial Roman climate. ' It would be an act of charity to solicit my liberation from the top of this mountain, where even the very air one breathes is frozen ; a truly fine sight to see everything four to five feet deep in snow, and the roofs so much covered that I cannot admit to having seen other walls than those in the interior of my

---

[1] Vide ch. ix.

habitation; the air is always thick, the winds everywhere prevail, and all is horror.'

On the southern side, where the town is surrounded by walls, the aspect is more genial, and the descent into the valley beneath is a mass of verdure. Here is the principal gate of the city, where side by side with the arms of the Republic appear those of its early protectors the Dukes of Urbino, outside which is a broad promenade called the ' *Stradone*,' where the inhabitants enjoy the favourite Italian game of ' *Pallone*,' a species of fives played with knuckledusters. Our republicans are by no means without a sense of merriment in their mountain retreat, nowhere are the privileges of the first of April more keenly appreciated. Whosoever on the morning of this day can be found in bed after sunrise, is liable to be dragged rudely from his couch, and adorned solely in his nocturnal toilette the wretched victim is placed on the back of a mule with an umbrella in his hand, and is conducted up and down the town, amidst the jangling of bells and the jeers of his persecutors, until at length he is allowed to return home to assume a garb more befitting the inclemency of the season, and the dictates of propriety; the gallant republicans however confine this punishment to sluggards of the male sex only.

The Città also contains a miniature theatre, and a museum at present not rich in antiquities, but possessing one eminently good picture by Giulio Romano, representing a holy family supported by SS. Marino and Agatha; formerly this was in the Council Chamber, but now, after being badly restored, it has been consigned to the museum, as a centre around which it is hoped other works of art will congregate.

The Belluzzi College of San Marino has a considerable local reputation; it was founded about two centuries ago, by a member of this illustrious Sammarinese family.

The nature of the soil all over the Republic is volcanic, deep gorges of tufa recall the neighbourhood of Vesuvius, and near Mongiardino much sulphur has been found, but not worked for want of capital. A good deal of marble, and many veins of coal and iron are also found,

and excellent building stone, which forms a
part of their restricted commerce. In fact, the
whole country represents a vast upheaval of
nature, to which probably is due the old name
of Mount Titanus, which was not changed till
some time after the saint had established his
community thereon; though some affirm, that
on this mountain was found a tomb, containing the skeleton of a giant, a soldier in
Pompey's army, and bearing on it the sole
epitaph ' Titanus.' Be this as it may, this was
the old name of the mountain, and this is still
a favourite name by which to call it, more
especially amongst the Italian eulogistic poets,
who sing the Republic's praises, and they are
not a few.

Having thus given the reader a rapid
glance at San Marino as it is, I purpose to look
into the historical incidents in its career, and
into its customs and constitutions, which it has
retained for so many centuries. The lapse of 250
years has made but little difference since Zuccoli,
writing in the early part of the seventeenth
century, took San Marino as the scene of one of

his dialogues, and entitled it '*La Città Felice*,' making a Belluzzi who was then a ' Captain ' of the Republic say, ' Our neighbours themselves do not clearly know the happiness of this Republic. At a distance, they only know us by name. Thus obscure to others we live as celebrities to ourselves, and, whilst others believe us to be wretched and miserable, we live content and comfortable together.'

CHAPTER II.

LEGENDARY HISTORY OF THE FOUNDATION OF THE REPUBLIC.

The commonwealth of Marino may boast at least of a nobler origin than that of Rome; the one having been at first an asylum for robbers and murderers, the other of persons eminent for piety and devotion.—Addison, *Travels in Italy.*

ALL history of Marinus, the founder of this Republic, is shrouded in mystery and legendary accounts. His life, and the miracles that he wrought, are written at length in the Book of the Acts of the Saints, and everything connected with his existence is as closely interwoven with the early history of this little state as that of Romulus was with the origin of Rome. Not only does the Republic bear his name, but it is lavishly distributed amongst the inhabitants at their baptism, and his statue occupies the most exalted place in their parish church. I will here transcribe, with unbiassed pen, the story of his life, and leave those who read to decide on the veracity of the same.

Early in the fourth century of the Christian era, the Emperor Diocletian decided on the rebuilding and repeopling of the ancient town of Ariminum, which afforded a good point of resistance to the impending barbaric invasions, and for this purpose exhorted all builders and hewers of stone thither to repair. Actuated by the spirit of enterprise, two youths set out on this invitation from the island of Arbi, on the opposite coast of Dalmatia, Marinus and Leo by name, 'leaving their parents, and sweet native fields; both of unbounded piety and wonderful eloquence and affability.'[1] To carry out the proposed fortifications the stone cutters had frequent recourse to Mons Titanus, to seek for stone where, as now, the products of the quarries were found to be excellent for building purposes.

A few years after their arrival Diocletian's

---

[1] *Acta Sanctorum die quarta Septembris.*

intolerant spirit was let loose on the Christians
within his Empire, and the fury of the persecu-
tion was felt nowhere more severely than at
Ariminum. Marinus, who is described as ' full of
manly vigour,' joined the persecuted Christians
in many of their conflicts against the Emperor's
proconsul and his men, fighting side by side
with the Christian Bishops of Forlì and Forlim-
popoli, and not unfrequently putting their
assailants to the rout. At length, weary of
this continued warfare, he and his friend Leo
betook themselves to Mons Titanus, where they
could hew their stones, and exercise their
religion unmolested. They planted a cross on
the summit of the rock, on which was inscribed
the sole word ' liberty,' and hewed themselves
beds beneath it, which are to be seen even now
behind the high altar of a small church devoted
to the purpose of protecting them, uncomfor-
table enough to our eyes, but sufficient for their
limited ideas of luxury. There are those who
maintain that these holes in the rock are merely
loculi, or catacombs; but the inhabitants of
San Marino are not of this opinion and affirm

the miracles wrought thereby to be not a few.

Numerous people assembled to hear the words of the saintly pair, and spread their fame afar. But other events had yet to occur to bring Marinus more conspicuously before the eyes of the world.

One Gaudentius was at this time Bishop o. Rimini, who, hearing of the virtue and merits of the two anchorites, summoned them to assist as deacons in his diocese. So for a time they left their solitude to mingle in the busy world of Rimini. About the year 360 A.D. the Christians were harassed by conflicting schisms, and a great council was held at Rimini. '400 bishops collected there, of whom but 80 were Arians; and the civil officers, to whom the Emperor Constantius had committed the superintendence of their proceedings, had orders not to let them stir out of the city till they should agree upon a confession of faith. . . . Distressed by their long confinement, impatient at their absence from their respective dioceses, and apprehensive of the approaching winter they began to waver. Thus ended the celebrated council the result of which is well characterized in the lively statement of Jerome, "the whole world groaned in astonishment to find itself Arian."[1]

Marinus himself took an active part in these debates; but his Arian enemies, not content with meeting him in the open field of argument, attacked our hermit with the insidious weapon of scandal.

Marcianus, an Arian bishop, so says the legend, placed a purse in the hands of a woman, Athleta by name, whose character was not altogether without reproach; she, in the public place of Rimini, before the assembled multitude, denounced Marinus as her lawful husband, affirming that she had travelled all the way from Dalmatia in quest of him. Marinus refuted the accusation with scorn and treated his accuser with pious contempt, whilst Athleta betook herself to the municipal authorities. Marinus, however, was unwilling to remain longer at Rimini, and, according to the *Acta*

[1] Newman, *The Arians of the Fourth Century.*

Sanctorum, 'was mindful of the text, " when
they may persecute you in one city flee unto
another," and, gathering himself together, fled
to Mount Titanus, and took up his abode in a
cave, where was a spring of water, and saw
not the face of man for twelve months, eat-
ing mountain herbs, and drinking water. The
devil raised up horrid animals to frighten him
at his devotions, but he persisted in his hymns
and songs night and day.'

By chance some swineherds, who were
attending their flocks, discovered his retreat, and
spread the report in Rimini. The injured
Athleta gave the peasants much money to point
out the spot, and thither went in person.
Marinus was in his garden gathering herbs
when she made her appearance, whereupon he
immediately entered his house and locked the
door, imbued with the spirit of S. Anthony, and
continued fasting and praying for six days;
whilst the woman, believing she had been
deceived by the devil, rushed back to Rimini
with great alarm, and was heard of no
more.

Our hermit, however, did not abandon his transactions with the fair sex after this bitter experience. There chanced to live a certain Roman widow, by name Felicissima, in the valley behind Mount Titanus. She not only owned a pleasant house situated in a lovely spot, but also most of the country around belonged to her, including the mountain, and her two sons served in the Emperor's guard. When once on a visit to their mother these two youths heard of the wonders wrought by Marinus, they forthwith set off, bow in hand, to rid the neighbourhood of so doubtful a character. Clambering up the mountain sides they came in sight of the hermit, when one of them, called Verissimo, stretched out his hand to shoot, and lo! his arm remained fixed so that he could not move it; terrified, they left Marinus in peace, and returned home. Felicissima, on seeing what had happened to her son, sent for the hermit to cure the injury he had caused; but before entering the house Marinus threw down all the images of Apollo and other gods, and then quietly proceeded to work his counter miracle, and received the blessings of the mother. Felicissima and her sons became converted on the spot, and the widow presented Marinus with his favourite mountain on which to form his community.

Here we have the legendary origin of the Republic, as it stands. Felicissima is now sanctified, and a small farm-house, belonging to the Franciscan Convent, professes to be built on the spot where once her villa stood, and the chimney-piece therein, which, by the way, differs little from those in the surrounding cottages, is said to date from her time, and consequently to work many miracles. At all events, a pilgrimage to her house would well repay the traveller, with the view that he there gets down the fertile valley of San Marino, and over the walls and towers which rise above him.

Marinus, it appears, frequently left his solitude to repair to the diocese in which he was deacon. One day on returning home, he found a bear had eaten his donkey. Nothing daunted he confronted the animal, and obliged it to assume the harness of the donkey and fulfil the menial duties of the domestic animal which it had eaten.

Meanwhile, after the Arian demonstration at Rimini, the orthodox few repaired to a spot a few miles distant from that town, and there established a small town, which still bears the name of '*La Cattolica*,' and now has a small station on the Brindisi line. Some, however, preferred to retire to Mount Titanus with their wives and families, and founded a religious community under the superintendence of Marinus. This community, however, was not based on the rules of monasticism; Marinus was no celibate, and encouraged matrimony amongst his followers; whether he himself ever entered into that state, recognizing the claim of Athleta, or eventually marrying the wealthy Felicissima, we are not told. At all events, the widow's name is often mentioned as assisting Marinus in his works of piety. His old fellow hermit, on the contrary, was raised to the episcopal dignity, and went with his followers to the neighbouring rock of Mons Feretri, where was an ancient temple to Jupiter Feretrius. Here

Leo established a purely ecclesiastical community, which soon became merged in the
country of the Montefeltri, a family whose name
is taken from this spot, a name inseparably connected with San Marino during the middle ages.
San Leo was one of their most impregnable fortresses, and we shall frequently be brought into
connection with it as the seat of the Bishops
of Feltria, the dread of the inhabitants of San
Marino during many succeeding centuries. An
excellent description of these twin fortresses
is given by Benvenuto da Imola in his commentary on Dante's line:

Vassi in San Leo descendesi in Nola.

Purg. cant. iv., v. 25.

'San Leo is a city of Romagna in Monte
Feltro, which at the time of our poet was
most desolate, and is now even more so. It
is situated on an extremely high mountain,
and surrounded on all sides by a very mountainous country; hence corn, and all things
necessary to sustain human life, are collected
within the fortifications. So also is the castle
of San Marino most strongly and ably fortified

by nature, about 4 miles distant from San Leo and 10 from Rimini (*sic.*) Hence Dante's simile is most apt; for his city of Purgatory resembles San Leo inasmuch as it is situated on a most lofty mountain, and only thinly populated, and, like San Leo, it is very strong, and free from treacherous assaults of an enemy.'

Marinus eventually died under the shadow of his adopted rock, and surrounded by his prosperous colony, to whom he had administered wise laws, and to whom his last dying words are reported to have been, ' I leave you free from all men.' He had refused to be raised to the dignity of a bishop like his colleague Leo, and was content to remain in deacon's orders. His body was buried on Mount Titanus, but was not suffered to rest long in peace; for in the year 752 A.D. Astolphus, king of the Lombards, carried it off to Pavia, where the Church of S. Michele still claims its possession, whereas the republicans say it was carefully restored to them by Pepin le Bref and is enclosed in a sarcophagus beneath the altar of his church. Every fourth of September

is a day held sacred to his memory, when, again
to quote the *Acta Sanctorum*, 'the venerable
treasure of his head is exposed to the admira-
tion, no less than the veneration, of the public.
For lo! it is seen preserved through centuries
from corruption, with some teeth, which, through
the life-like brightness of the gums which join
them, fall little short of the teeth of living
people.'

Numerous are the inducements for the
inhabitants of the Republic to bear in mind the
history of their saint. Over the portal of their
parish church is written, in large letters, this
inscription:

Divo Marino, Patrono et Libértatis Auctori, S.P.R.Q.

Over the high altar a statue of the saint
superintends the devotions of his admirers,
beautifully executed in white marble by
Taddolini of Bologna, a worthy pupil of
Canova's; he is represented as dressed in his
deacon's robes, with a scroll in his hand in which
is written ' *Libertas.*'

The modern parish church is handsome, but

contains nothing worthy of remark; externally
built after the fashion of a Corinthian Temple,
the Campanile is all that is left of the old edifice,
which was probably amongst the oldest Christian

PARISH CHURCH.

buildings in Italy, dating from 1126, and which
was originally dedicated to S. Peter. The
present building was opened in 1855 by the
Bishop of Montefeltro, who shares with the

Bishop of Rimini the spiritual supervision of the Sammarinesi.

'A l'ombre du 'nom de son saint patron protégée par son peu d'importance San Marino a subsisté jusqu' à nous, et nous montre cette alliance de la religion et de la liberté qui fut le caractère des communes italiennes au xiiie siècle. Rien ne saurait exprimer plus vivement une telle alliance que la nouvelle cathédrale de Saint Marin. Les sept milles habitants qui forment la population de ce petit état, et qui payent un impôt annuel de quatre sous par tête, sont parvenus à bâtir de leurs économies une fort belle église qui a coûté 150,000 francs.'[1]

Around the columns of the church all the inhabitants are buried, no cemetery having yet been required; when the place is full the bones are removed to a charnel-house, under the front colonnade, the simple mountaineers believing that they will rest more secure under the immediate shadow of their country's god.

Great is the veneration in which S. Marino is held, and the fines for taking his name in

[1] Ampère.

D

vain are made higher than those for blasphem-
ing any other saint ; for the wise lawgivers of this
Republic attempt to check the mouths of those
who wish to swear by a descending scale of
penalties.

Two officials are annually appointed by the
State to see that no harm may happen to any of
the relics of the saint, and are called ' Massarii.'

On the fourth of September the Sammarinesi
hold a grand *festa* to his honour, when, after
the routine of the morning's Mass, the procession, and the exposure of the relics have
been successfully concluded, they assemble in a
wide open space called 'La Fratta,' between
two of the towers, a part, says Oreste Brizi,
' reclaimed from the screech-owl by a later
extension of the walls.' Here they indulge
themselves in all kinds of games, shooting and
various gymnastic exercises. These are often
followed by a game, which is happily now said
to be dying out, and only occurs on the day
of the patron saint ; for be their virtues many
in other respects, these Republicans would not
bear the inspection of a committee upon cruelty

to animals. A live cock is procured, and hung from a piece of wood about nine feet from the ground. Then each player advances in turn to a spot marked out, from whence by a leap he tries to grasp and pull off the bird's neck; if he succeeds he wins the cock, and comes back amidst loud applause, if not he pays a trifle to the owner, and receives the hisses of the spectators.

By proceeding outside the walls, many other points in connection with the legends of San Marino are brought before the notice of the curious; a steep rocky cliff forms one side of a rounded hill called Montalbo, by climbing which with the aid of hands and knees, a curious spot is reached about half-way up, which is called the garden of S. Marino. Here, report says, he used to shelter himself from the winds, and, though bare of vegetation all round, on this spot may be seen some sprigs of laurel, which does not grow elsewhere in a like position; and over the grotto, where he used to sleep, hang festoons of ivy, whilst sweet smelling herbs and pinks grow just below. A visit to this place is considered as most efficacious in all cases of fever. Surely it must be accounted far more miraculous, if an invalid pilgrim arrives safely at the foot of the treacherous path, which overlooks a yawning precipice, and has only a few feet of precarious foothold.

A small hamlet belonging to the Republic has grown up round a well, where the saint used to ' baptize his converts, springing from underneath a cliff. The name of the village is Acqua Viva, which records the fact, and is a favourite spot for the growth of the S. Giovese grape, which produces a rich sparkling wine, one of the best in the locality.

Though S. Marino cannot rival other saints as a favourite subject for the pencil of Italian artists, yet there is an excellent picture by Guercino in the possession of Signor Settimio Belluzzi in the Borgo, representing our saint with beautifully flowing hoary locks, dressed as a deacon, holding in one hand a plan of the small Republic and its towers, whilst in the other he is giving the benediction.

The light thrown on this picture, and the

expression of the face, are amongst the most
effective this master has produced.

A Sammarinese artist has painted a picture,
which hangs under the dais of the throne in the
Council Chamber, representing the founder of
the Republic in the garb of an anchorite, and
pointing to the words, which he has just
chiselled in the rock, 'Relinquo vos ab omnibus
liberi.' It is more from the fact that this
picture seems to overlook every action of the
Government than from its artistic merit that it
claims the attention of the visitor.

A vast series of hideous mezzo-tinto productions, describing the various incidents in S.
Marino's mythical career, adorn a large room
below, but are fortunately placed too high to
be closely criticized, and the light is bad.

Such is the legendary history of San Marino,
which, thanks to their spiritual advisers, the
Sammarinesi devoutly believe; yet it is impossible to help admiring their attachment to
all that is connected with their early founder,
and the liberty which they so dearly prize.

CHAPTER III.

EARLY GLIMPSES AT SAN MARINO'S EXISTENCE.

COMPLEX as the history of Italy is throughout, and divided as it has been into so many and numerous towns and communities, each with a history of its own, yet none of which can be properly understood without reference to the others, it is refreshing to take up a position on the rocks of Mount Titanus, from which so much of the outer world can be contemplated, whilst the internal history proceeds in as peaceable a groove as fifteen troublous centuries would allow.

San Marino has passed quietly through its phases of a hermitage, a sanctuary, a castle, and a republic, surrounded on all sides by some of the most stirring scenes of Italian history. Situated as it was in the Exarchate of Ravenna,

and consequently forming part of Pepin's donation to the Holy See, its early history dates
from those times when the foreign element
brought disasters and calamities into the peninsula, before the infant efforts at independence,
built on the dying embers of the Roman Empire, had time to develope and become mature.

To the early invaders of Italian soil, rocky
desolation like that around Mount Titanus was
no temptation. Whilst the fair cities of the
plains were rifled again and again by barbaric
hordes, these hill-set sanctuaries escaped, owing
to their poverty and insignificance ; and it is
not until the events which arose out of the
Lombard invasion of the Exarchate, that we
find San Marino mentioned in the pages of
history.

For a period of two hundred years Italy
was unequally divided between the kingdom of
the Lombards and the Exarchate of Ravenna,
whilst Rome was degraded into a city of the
second rank. The earlier Exarchs governed
Italy in the name of the Eastern Empire with
some degree of power, but after the days of

Narses their jurisdiction became much limited. The modern Romagna, and the marshes and valleys of Ferrara and Comachio, with a maritime *Pentapolis* as far south as Ancona, and an inland one which vaguely extended to the Apennines, formed the nucleus of the Exarchate. Some other provinces recognised this supremacy, whilst the rest of Italy was entirely under the Lombard rule.

Romagna, as a name for this district, was curiously applied, rather to imply the power of the Holy Roman Empire, as represented by the Exarchs, than as later writers would have it, from its immediate connection with Rome, as part of the disputed territory given to the hierarchy. For here the country is far less Italian than on the western slopes of the Apennines. The Senonian Gauls have left their name here in *Sinigaglia*, whilst the Greeks gave a name to Ancona, and San Marino and San Leo owe their origin to Dalmatian emigrants; and to this day the dialect of Romagna partakes more of the brusqueness of the north, for by leaving out the final syllable of each word, the

R)magnan peasant would appear to speak more of a French than an Italian patois. A Sammarinese of to-day will say ' *demain* ' instead of ' *domani* ' for ' to-morrow,' with almost a Parisian accent.

When, in A.D. 752, the Lombards under Astolphus wrested the Exarchate from the Eastern Empire, a new era was introduced into Italy, and a series of conflicting elements for centuries to come. The Popes groaned in their weakness to see the aggrandisement of the Lombard race, and were unable to obtain any succour from the East, where the Emperor Constantine Copronymus cared little and could do less for his Western feudatory. Stephen II. was led to call in the aid of Pepin, and introduce that foreign element so proverbially disastrous to the Italian.

The Lombard king Astolphus had deprived San Marino of the bones of its patron saint, so esteemed at that time was the worship of the hermit; but when conquered by Pepin, he was obliged to return them from his Church of San Michele at Pavia, where they had been

deposited, at the same time that the district of
Romagna was presented to the Holy See. It
appears that in this donation Pepin entirely
ignored the rightful sovereign at Constanti-
nople, but handed over the conquered Pentapolis, as says the chronicler of Stephen II., ' to
the Church of Rome, represented by pontiffs,
and to the Republic of Rome,' which probably
referred to the local government of the Eternal
City. But this present remained a gift only in
name. Twenty-two towns, including the ' *Castel
San Mariano*,' which from the position can be
none other than our rock, deposited their keys
on the altar of St. Peter ; but the Popes never
enjoyed the sovereignty over these provinces,
over which the Bishops of Ravenna continued
to exercise a nominal sway, whilst each town
exercised its own form of government, without
any exterior interference.

Documents about the existence of San
Marino are about this period exceedingly
scanty. We find a monk, Eugippius, who
lived at San Leo, recording the existence of a
pious man, Basilico, who was one of the imme-

diate successors of Marinus; and again, we read in the life of Stephen II., that San Marino fought against Astolphus, incorporated as it was in the Exarchate. But it is not for two centuries later that we come across any very authentic testimony to its existence as a community.

It was reserved for Charlemagne to free the Papacy eventually from its dangerous enemies, the Lombard chiefs. The great Frankish Emperor received his diadem from the hands of the Popes, and confirmed the donation his father had made. But the Carlovingian supremacy is a sorry page in the history of Italy. Excessive corruption and social misery mark this period, which culminated in 888 in the dastardly reign of Charles the Fat; and when the Frankish Empire came to an end in Italy on the death of this monarch, all that it can be said to have done for Italy was to have introduced three new ideas—firstly, the temporal power of the Church; secondly, the supremacy of the West-ern Empire, as represented by a Northern power; and thirdly, vassalage—all of which in

the centuries to come tended to exhaust the
very life-blood of the peninsula.

Meanwhile, around the relics of San Marino,
a family was taking root under whose shelter
this small community even then reposed; but
this connection is illustrated during the Dark
Ages only by one solitary manuscript quoted
by Muratori. The House of Montefeltro in
their earliest origin was represented by one
Duke Orso, and the cloak of San Leo had fallen
on one Giovanni, Bishop of Montefeltro. Together the duke and bishop watched over the
interests of San Marino, and allowed Stephen,
the abbot of that place, to hold his funds and
revenues, and to exercise his jurisdiction against
the encroachments of one Deltone, then Bishop
of Rimini. This proves to us that at this time
our Republic existed only as a canonic corpora-
tion, and that it was under the temporal protection of the House of Montefeltro, and under
the spiritual protection of its bishops. Of this
Duke Orso the annals of the House of Feltria
are silent, and it is not known whether he
was a lineal ancestor of the Dukes of Urbino or ·

no. But his existence is attested by an inscription around the baldacchino of the baptismal font in the Cathedral of San Leo, which records that it was presented by Duke Orso in the year 882. The document in question is entitled the '*Placito Feretrano*,' and is dated

CATHEDRAL OF SAN LEO.

February 20, 885, and is the first reliable proof of the existence of our infant Republic.

During this century the intimate connection between the Teutonic and Latin elements was being firmly cemented in Rome,[1] schools

[1] Ranke's *History of the Popes.*

being opened in the Eternal City for Frieslanders and Saxons; and as the empire of the Franks fell into decay, the Popes, in the utmost adversity, had to look elsewhere for support. When the great Lombard Duchy of Benevento and the Duchies of Spoleto and Tuscany ceased to have weight in the affairs of Italy, Berenger, Marquis of Friuli for thirty-six years, established a transitory standpoint for Italian independence; but after his death calamities fell thick and fast on Italian soil. The Saracens invaded the southern coasts, whilst the Hungarians laid waste the plains of Lombardy, and Berenger II., the then reigning sovereign of Italy, was content to hold his throne as a feudatory of the Teuton Emperor Otho I.

In common with the rest of Italy, San Marino began to see the necessity of building walls, and collecting the nucleus of the population in one common centre. We are told that the strong fortifications on the western side of Mount Titanus owe their origin to Berenger himself, but none of the traces of these early constructions now remain, all the walls bearing the character of a later date, and were probably built by Federigo, the great Duke of Urbino,[1] who took a special interest in San Marino's welfare, and whose eagle is placed side by side with the three towers of the Republic on the principal gateway.

Be this as it may, when Otho visited Italy to chastise his refractory vassal for some disturbance which had occurred, Berenger chose San Marino as a standpoint on which to rally his fallen fortunes, and from the summit of Mount Titanus issued a diploma on October 7, 951, which he signed as 'made in the community of San Marinus,' and this forms a second testimony to the early history of our state.

But Berenger soon fell a sacrifice to the victorious arms of Otho, and was carried prisoner into Germany; and the Teuton Emperor took an early opportunity to depose the Pope John XII., who had solicited the German aid, and received the imperial diadem in 961 from Pope Leo, whom the Emperor had raised to

[1] Chapter viii.

the chair of St. Peter in his stead. In the following year we find Otho dealing out portions
of his newly-acquired territory to faithful vassals, and, amongst others, the Count Uldarico
of Carpegna was presented with twenty-eight
castles and land 'between the rivers *Conca* and
Marichium, Serravalle, San Marino, and the
town of Mons Feretri (San Leo).' This is probably the origin of the House of Montefeltro,
as we shall see in the ensuing chapter, and the
cause of its firm adherence to Ghibelline interests.

The spirit of this century is generally marked
by the growing power of the nobles; the frequent barbarian incursions obliged the cities to
offer citizenship to the neighbouring barons in
return for the assistance of their armed troops,
thereby laying up a store of tyranny for themselves in the times to come. Thus the Malatesti
found their way into Rimini, the Visconti
into Milan, and all those lordly houses, which
were hereafter inseparably connected with the
cities, which adopted them. The want of roads
and communication between city and city made

each dependent on its own internal resources, whilst all united in common respect and homage to the clergy, and round each sacred fane the scattered inhabitants of the country gathered like flocks of sheep. In no other country but Italy could so many centres of civilization have so spontaneously arisen. Each city was a little *Rome* for the surrounding district, rising up, so to speak, out of the embers of ancient civilization; each community was prepared to exercise its own jurisdiction and issue codes of laws based on Justinian, whilst the executive authority was generally placed in the hands of consuls whose election was due to the body of the people at large. Amongst countless contemporaries the ' *community of the Castle of San Marino,*' as it is styled in the earliest manuscripts, was in those days as equitably governed as now, and with a constitution which has hardly undergone any change during the lapse of centuries.

But events in the following century were to occur which would entirely remodel the state of Italian society at large. It was the Papacy, not the Empire, which was to effect this change. A series of weak pontiffs, who fawned on the German emperors on one side and the Norman invaders on the other, held the chair of St. Peter, elected by the stronger Roman princes, or by women who ruled in the Eternal City with the spirit of Faustina; whilst the German emperors from time to time held their diets at Roncaglia, and were content if their feudatories periodically swore fealty there.

But on the accession of Henry III. to the imperial throne, whilst still a minor, the Papal chair was occupied by the indomitable Hildebrand. Then began that suicidal contest between Pope and Emperor which stained the fair fields of Italy with the blood of civil war for three centuries. To reform the internal state of the Church was Gregory the VII.'s first care, by establishing celibacy and checking the gross immorality amongst the clergy; then by declaring the Empire elective he enrolled the aristocratic interests in Germany on his side, and was enabled to strike his final blow by asserting that the Church had the sole right of nomination to vacant sees, and that the Tiara

was supreme over all earthly crowns. How
the Papal efforts were furthered by the Countess
Matilda of Tuscany, and how Henry was obliged
to do penance at her castle of Canossa, near
Parma, to the vindictive Pope ; how Henry by
his indomitable courage so far recouped his fortunes as to threaten his rival in the very castle
of St. Angelo, until he was repulsed by Robert
Guiscard the Norman, and barely escaped with
life through the territories of the Countess
Matilda to Germany, from whence during the
remainder of his reign he no longer dared to
come down on the plains of Italy ;—all these
are incidents well known in history, which bore
their fruits in the coming century, and they
were threefold : the Normans succeeded in
firmly establishing themselves in the districts of
Naples and Sicily, Central Italy became nominally under the sovereignty of the Popes, whilst
the cities of Lombardy and Northern Italy, far
from any central form of government, gradually
established themselves as free communities.
Some time previous the germs of freedom had
taken root at Milan ; taking advantage of the

feuds between the lesser and greater barons, the inhabitants, under the guidance of one Lanzone, established the commune of Milan, and with it one of the first banners which shook the power of the Empire. The towns thus freed from the thraldom of tyranny began to show signs of that brilliancy in art and literature which was to make them for ever illustrious ; securely shut in within the city walls, the artizans had no longer cause to fear the incursions of invading arms, and opportunity was given them to expand their incipient talents. Again, the period of the Crusades contributed much to the development of this tendency. Not only was Italy favoured by climate and situation as a magazine from which to furnish supplies and a passage for the troops, when eastward bound, but also they were brought by this means into more immediate contact with the East, where civilization was more advanced. Again, the scourge of Italian soil was the constant petty warfare of the smaller nobles, who by means of the Crusades were drafted away in the retinues of their feudal superiors, most of them never to return.

Thus at this time we find Milan, as the representative of this spirit of freedom, openly defying the dictates of the emperors, sacrificing at the same time their weaker neighbours to their spirit of ambition, which proved how rotten was their Liberal government—a tyranny in all but name.

. In 1158, the imperial throne was at length filled by a man of energy and ambition, Frederic Barbarossa, who was not content to see his influence in Italy fall into decay; he crossed the Alps and descended on the town of Milan, on which he imposed a *Podestà*, which forms the first instance of that curious introduction of a foreign element to assist in the government, which now alone exists on the summit of Mount Titanus.[1] The independence of Italy, however, had taken too deep a root to be thus easily crushed, and the formation of the Lombard League united all the free cities of Northern Italy, from the Alps as far south as Ancona, in one common cause against the Teuton. In the year 1167, twenty-four cities were joined

[1] *Vide* chapter xiv.

together at the town of Bergamo by this League, the results of which were manifested in 1176 by the victory of Legnano, when Barbarossa found himself defeated by the instrumentality of those very men of Milan on whom ten years before he had imposed all the horrors of conquest.

But this spirit of independence expired, extinguished by the force of this its last breath ; for instead of taking advantage of the opportunity afforded them by the Peace of Constance, the Lombard cities gave way to that spirit of selfish ambition which Milan had before exhibited, and the fair plant of liberty was gradually left to perish on Italian soil, where everything else that was beautiful took root and flourished. The glories of the Peace of Constance passed away from Italy like a waning star, and after it arose a dark period of social slavery, illumined only by the false brilliancy of art and luxury, a state of refinement which never developed itself on the slopes of San Marino, which remains an oasis to this day in the midst of a land overflowing with objects of grandeur, grand alone in the possession of its ancient freedom. The inhabitants of Mount Titanus during these stirring times offer us a singular example of peace and contentment. Conscious of their weakness, they made no attempt to extend their territories by force of arms, but contracted for themselves two purchases of lands from their neighbours and protectors, the Counts of Carpegna, one in A.D. 1100, and the other, seventy years later, of the lands of Penna Rossa and Casoli. Curiously enough, these documents of sale are both signed by notaries of the same name, affording an instance in these early times of the frequent recurrence of the same name in the same office, as now, looking down a list of captains for the last fifty years, one cannot fail to be struck with the frequency with which the name of Belluzzi or Bonelli occur.

About this time the immediate neighbours of San Marino became more conspicuous in the pages of history, and without a sketch of their rivalries and factions it will be impossible to understand the position held by our Republic.

placed as it was in the very jaws of each. For
in the words of an old commentator on Dante,
Benvenuto Rimaldo by name: ' In these neighbouring mountains sprang up three families
amongst the most potent tyrants of Italy, that
of the Feltria, Malatesti, and Faggiuoli; but if in
these mountains, in the bosom of anarchy, the
seed of tyranny sprang up, on the summit of
one of them alone could liberty save itself from
the general shipwreck, and maintain itself free
and independent amongst two rival despots who
hedged them in.'

CHAPTER IV.

SOME OF SAN MARINO'S MORE IMMEDIATE
NEIGHBOURS.

'Questo è un sito così erto, sì scosceso, e sì forte, che la poca gente non può farvi su disegno, e la molta non vi si può ne accostare ne maneggiare.'—ZUCCOLI, *Dialogo della Città felice.*

AFTER the peace of Constance the history of Italy is the history of the rise of despotism in a thousand different forms ; a state of society well calculated to sharpen men's intelligence, as is amply testified by the rapid growth of art in this atmosphere. The frequent changes in government made each man feel dependent on his own resources, not only for a livelihood, but for life. Members of the same family were ranged on opposite sides, and the Italian of those days lived his life, left a distinguished name, and died before a modern character has

reached an age of full development. By contrasting San Marino with the rest of Italy, we
get this idea brought more forcibly before us.
Here the government was always the same, for
the inhabitants of Mount Titanus were seldom
internally affected by the scenes around them,
and the striking contrast now exhibited by San
Marino to the rest of Italy at once suggests the
thought that, if Italy had all along been independent under a settled government, and no foreign
elements had been brought to bear upon it,
we should never have heard of the names of
Raphael and his fellows, nor have had the
stately structures with which each town is decorated to admire. For the Sammarinesi were
men of the same kindred as the men of Urbino
or Bologna, but the school of life which they
have passed through has been different.

Let us now take a glance at some of San
Marino's more immediate neighbours.

Firstly, under the slopes of the mountain of
Carpegna we find a hardy race of nobles, who
vaunted that they could trace their origin to
Justinian, as is attested by a stone put over the

gateway of the Franciscan convent at San Marino, which, with flattering respect, represents
the head of Justinian placed side by side with
the eagle of Montefeltro. Be this as it may, in
the twelfth century the House of Carpegna was
represented by three branches—the Counts of
Carpegna, who continued to hold their mountain fief in utter insignificance till 1815, when
the Camera Apostolica bought from them their
sovereign jurisdiction for 65,000*l.*, and next
day sold it for one-fifteenth of that sum. The
other two branches being eventually combined,
gradually waxed strong in their Ghibelline
interests, presenting to Italy a noble race of
warriors, until Antonio di Carpegna, espousing
warmly the cause of Frederic Barbarossa in
1154, received as his reward the castles and
land around San Leo, with the title of Count of
Montefeltro, a title representing at the same
time the old temple of Jupiter Feretri on Monte
Feltria, and the nucleus of their strength in the
fortress of San Leo.

Secondly, on the side of Rimini, we find
the House of Malatesta, or the ‘wrongheads,’

as they were justly called, claiming their origin from Scipio, and early established in the neighbouring stronghold of Verucchio, probably an offshoot of this same family of Carpegna, who derived their name from some personal appearance. This race is chiefly renowned in history for the able warriors it produced, celebrated no less for their perfidy and cruelty than for their prowess in war. But they never succeeded in extending their territories far, or forming any strong basis of power; for they never established a system of primogeniture like their neighbours in Urbino, and consequently their lands became divided amongst numerous branches. This House of Malatesta was early summoned from Verucchio by the inhabitants of Rimini to protect them against the northern incursions, and when established there commenced a system of tyranny which was but slightly compensated for by their patronage of the arts. Their position as head of the Guelphic faction in Romagna brought them in constant hostile connection with the House of Feltria, a fact which, in a measure, assisted the inhabitants of San Marino to maintain their independence, since Mount Titanus formed a natural bulwark between the two.

Again, a third neighbour, whose insidious attempts on our Republic's freedom furnish us with an excellent specimen of mediæval life, was the Bishop of Montefeltro, who governed under the Counts the spiritual affairs of this district. From their see at San Leo the Bishops attempted in every way to usurp political power, thereby displaying the characteristic of their age. Whilst the Popes aimed at universal power, these lesser stars strove hard to shine in their respective spheres. Messer Ugolino, Bishop of Montefeltro during a greater part of the thirteenth century, was a man of the times. By a dexterous manipulation of the quarrels around him, he was generally to be found on the winning side. He followed the standard of the Counts of Montefeltro during the time of the ascendancy of Ghibellinism, but on the defeat of the latter he took an early opportunity of reconciling himself with the Pope. He purchased a house on Mount Titanus, and was very officious in lending his aid to the republicans in all their legal quarrels and purchases, and was only prevented by an opportune death from assuming entire signoral rights over San Marino. His conduct formed a precedent for his successors; but the Sammarinesi grew wise through experience, and always received the blandishments of their spiritual lords with distrust. But this is anticipating the thread of our history.

In the year 1186 a marriage took place between Henry VI. of Germany and Constance, heiress of the Norman line of princes in Sicily, by which means the House of Swabia was raised to its zenith on both sides of the Alps. This union was, however, of short duration, for both died a few years afterwards, and left an infant son, Frederic II., whose long minority was placed under the supervision of Pope Innocent III., a pontiff who equalled Hildebrand in his struggles for aggrandising the Holy See. For fifty years after Frederic's accession, Italy was the scene of constant struggle between Pope and Emperor. City was divided against city

and brother against brother ; but still the contest had a meaning, and the name of Guelph
and Ghibelline was not an idle pretext for a
brawl, as it became towards the close of the
thirteenth century.

Buonconte, the head of the House of Feltria,
fought well for his imperial master, and fighting under his banner we find the Bishop of
Montefeltro and the Men of San Marino constantly enumerated. Thus, when, during the
pontificates of Gregory IX. and Innocent IV.,
the thunders of excommunication were issued
against the Empire and its adherents, we find
the simple men of San Marino also under this
ban. But Ugolino, the bishop, had made his
peace with the Church before, and was able to
effect a reconciliation for the unpretending
mountaineers, who were reblessed in the Church
of Perugia ; and a few years later we find
Mount Titanus chosen as a sort of neutral
ground, on which the contending parties assembled for a conference, at the instigation of
Philip, Bishop of Ravenna. As another mark
of peace and prosperity during these turbulent

times, we find the Sammarinesi making a further purchase of land from Taddeo, Count of
Montefeltro, in 1253, of the hamlet of Casoli.
This sale was supervised by Giovanni, Bishop
of Montefeltro, who had succeeded Ugolino
both in his see and in his endeavours to obtain
a footing on Mount Titanus through blandishments. At this time also we find San Marino
offering a retreat to those who, through politics
or misfortune, found their homes too hot for
them. Thus the Parcitadi, the one Ghibelline
family at Rimini, had to fly from the victorious
Malatesti. They were received with open arms
by our Republic, with a pleasant pun on their
name, referring to their loss of citizenship.

Meanwhile the hostilities between Pope and
Emperor went on with increasing vigour. So
implacable was Gregory IX. to his rival, that
when Frederic II. gave up his European con-
tests to fight the Church's battles in the East,
the old Pope followed him with his excommunications, declaring him a 'piratical captain,'
and thereby putting an effectual check to any
success over the infidel. When, therefore, in

1245, Frederic was deposed at the Council of
Lyons, the Papacy fulfilled the dream of Hildebrand, and for a time the triumph of the spiritual arms was complete. Frederic died in
1250, leaving a heritage of warfare to his son
Conrad, who fought bravely for four years
against the arms of Innocent in Naples, the
Pope claiming that country as forfeited to the
Holy See ; and then Manfred, his illegitimate
brother, carried on the defence of his patrimony with consummate bravery, until the
Popes called in other aid, and produced further
complications on Italian soil.

The age of Frederic II., however, did not pass
away without leaving its footprints in Italy. By
introducing the system of mercenaries, a new
era was commenced, not only for Italy but for
the rest of Europe, whilst the Italian nobles
traded in warfare and hired themselves out as
condottieri. France followed Frederic's example
by establishing a paid army of Saracens, and by
employing Swiss and Scottish guards in their service. Many of these Italian *condottieri* realised
by their prowess large fortunes, and not behind

F

the rest was the house of the Feltrians, who
spent large sums in beautifying Urbino, Gubbio,
and other towns under their jurisdiction, and
in mitigating the miseries of their subjects,
whilst other less liberal-minded autocrats used
it only as a means to grind down their people
for their own further aggrandisement.

During the latter half of this century, the
parties of Guelph and Ghibelline ceased to exist
in anything but name. Every city was divided
by wretched feuds, this or some other more
appropriate name being adopted, according to
circumstances. Amongst the cities of Romagna, Bologna stands out as a prominent
example, whose contending parties adopted the
name of the Gieremei and Lambertazzi, the
origin of their feud being a romantic story, told
as follows by Sismondi :[1] 'Imalda, a noble lady
of the Ghibelline house of Lambertazzi, chanced
to fall in love with Bonifaccio, a scion of the
Guelphic house of Gieremei, and at one of their
clandestine interviews the brothers of Imalda fell
on Bonifaccio and wounded him with a poisoned

[1] Sismondi, *History of Italian Republics.*

dagger. Imalda, who had effected an escape, returned shortly to the spot where the body of her lover lay still warm, and hopeful still to restore him, she sucked the wound, and the poison was thus communicated to her veins. Side by side the two lovers lay dead; and, exasperated by the sight, the two rival families fought for very existence, but finally the Lambertazzi were driven from the city. 12,000 citizens were banished, and their houses razed.'

The Count Guido di Montefeltro put himself at the head of the fugitives, and in their command acquired that reputation for being a 'grand captain,' which has been immortalised by Dante in his divine comedy. The history of Count Guido is one which in all the turmoil of the century would have sunk into insignificance, if it had not been for Dante's love of Romagna and the Feltrian race. He introduces Buonconte amongst his characters in Purgatory, and Count Guido he finds in the bottomless pit itself; and it is in relating their history, and in talking kindly to poor Guido to assuage his woes, that

Dante gives us so excellent an epitome of the history of Romagna at this time, a history which bears so strongly on the welfare of San Marino, that it cannot be passed unnoticed.

The Umbrian Mountains' were amongst Dante's favourite haunts when exiled from his native Florence. The monastery of St. Croce d'Avellana, near Cagli, he chose as his ideal of a spot for prayer, at the foot of Monte Catria, where the savage aspect of nature forms indeed a spot calculated to evoke mystic wanderings in a fantastic brain. The rocky San Leo he chose as a fitting simile for his entrance into purgatory, and his infernal regions are thickly peopled with characters from this district, a doubtful compliment indeed, but one which has served to give many of these worthies a celebrity they would otherwise not have had. Hence we find in Dante not only a beautifier and re-modeller of the Italian vernacular, but also a valuable historian of the facts which went on around him, for in his early days he had fought under the banner of Guido di Montefeltro, whom he styles 'the honour of Romagna,' under the walls

of Pisa, perhaps side by side with 'the men of
San Marino,' who followed the same standard
for weal or woe, when the Ghibelline interests

CASTLE OF VERRUCHIO.

were at stake. From the summit of Mount
Titanus the towers of Verruchio rise up on a
neighbouring height, where Paolo and Francesca
da Rimini paid the penalty of their illicit love.

Guido di Montefeltro was one of those restless spirits which mark the age, whose assistance
kept the fast decaying Ghibelline power alive.
When the Popes, anxious to overthrow the
Swabian house in Naples, called in the aid of
Charles of Anjou, the triumph of the Guelphs
was almost complete. The French influence
and the French arms seemed destined for ever
to sever the slender thread which bound Italy
to the Roman Emperors. Conradin, the last of
his house, suffered for his adherence to his ancestral rights on the scaffold, and Charles of Anjou,
placed as he was at the head of the Guelphs,
was in a position to dictate his own terms in the
peninsula. We find one Giovanni d'Appia or
d'Epa, a Frenchman acting as Martin IV.'s
legate in Romagna, in constant warfare with
Count Guido, who conquered him near Cervia,

> The city which made the long resistance,
> And of the French a sanguinary heap.—DANTE, *Inferno.*
> LONGFELLOW.

At length, however, Guido was routed, and for
a time took up his residence on Mount Titanus.
But his spirit could not long rest quiet, and

though vanquished by Rome, and his sons held
as hostages by the Pontiff, we again find him
leading the Pisans against the Florentines, until
at length, wearied by the troubles of the world
and imbued with the fanaticism of the age, he
took the cowl in 1296, and became a follower
of St. Francis, the pious monk of Assisi, who
at the beginning of this century had struck at
the very root of the rottenness of the Church,
and had brought about, by his zealous en- •
deavours, that revival which gave the hierarchy
a new base of existence, so to speak, and postponed the days of Luther for centuries. But
Guido's disposition was not suited for a cell; at
the instigation of Boniface VIII., he left his
seclusion to fight the battles of the successor of
that Pontiff against whom he had before borne
arms, so versatile were the politics of the day.
The regrets he felt for this are thus echoed by
Dante from his tomb :

> I was a man of arms, then Cordelier,
> Believing thus begirt to make amends,
> And truly, my belief had been fulfilled
> But for the high priest, whom may ill betide,
> Who put me back into my former sins.

Guido eventually died in the odour of sanctity,
A.D. 1299.

Politics in Romagna at this time give us an
insight into the conditions of the family of this
age. On the so-called Guelphic side we find
Paolo, son of Da Verruchio, the great Malatesta
of Rimini, the ancient mastiff of Dante,

> Who made such bad disposal of Romagna,

at the head of affairs, supported by the exiles
from San Marino and other Ghibelline places,
and by Taddeo di Montefeltro, whilst Guido at
the head of the Ghibellines was assisted by
Ramberto Malatesta, the exiles of Rimini, and
the men of San Marino. The characters of these
two leading chiefs are admirably summed up by
Dante, who spoke of Malatesta as above, whilst
he thus puts it into Guido's mouth to say,

> The deeds I did
> Were not those of a lion, but a fox ;
> The machinations, and the covert ways,
> I knew them all, and practised so their craft,
> That to the ends of earth the sound went forth.

When in 1283 the Sicilian Vespers startled the
world with the most atrocious outrage of those

dark ages, the French element in the South received a shock from which it never recovered. Constance, the sole survivor of the Swabian house, carried with her to Spain the claims of her family to the two Sicilies; hence we find a new vulture hovering round to claim its share of the corpse of Italy. Meanwhile the House of Austria was reviving the strength of the Empire by the infusion of new blood; Rudolph, the first of the Hapsburgs, acquired more active authority than his predecessors, and by afresh conferring the donations of Pepin and Charlemagne, kept alive the flame of the German element in Italy, which was now almost extinct.

But in Romagna a transient peace was in store at the close of the thirteenth century. In 1299 a cessation of hostilities was proclaimed, and at the convention for this purpose San Marino was represented by Count Galeazzo, then at the head of the House of Feltria. Thus it was that Dante consoled the anxious shade of Guido,

Romagna thine is not, and never has been,
Without war in the bosom of its tyrants;
But open war I none have left there now.

During the weakness of the House of Feltria for the ensuing century, we shall find our Republic struggling for its very existence with the emissaries of the Popes. The Pontiffs themselves, however, had not the opportunity of superintending their own affairs in Italy, and it was only to further their own ambitious ends that the legates acted thus. For with the death of Boniface VIII. the power of the Papacy was temporarily at an end. Hildebrand, Innocent III., and Boniface VIII., had stretched its power to the utmost, and men ceased to fear their anathemas ; and when in 1305 Clement V. was induced to remove his Court to Avignon, the Popes were for the next seventy years but a tool in the hands of France.

CHAPTER V.

DIFFICULTIES WITH PAPAL LEGATES.

La République de San Marino n'est ni redoutée, ni re-
doutable, telle est la cause de sa longue prospérité.—F. DE
BARGHON-FORTRION.

THE story of San Marino for the centuries to
come has a firmer basis on which to stand. The
documents relating to it are more consecutive
and precise, and can be freed from any suspicion of being but legendary lore. Thus we
find the consuls assuming the name of Captains.
The '*Palazzo Pubblico*' was built, the Borgo
became considered as the natural centre of
commerce, and the Sammarinesi felt prepared
to meet the honours of self-government with
fitting respectability. For previously to this,
self-government was a natural state of affairs,
even in the smallest communities; but now that
every town had selected its ruling family, or

become known as a flourishing republic, San Marino found itself isolated, and consequently accepted its position as such. The Council was in the habit of altering their statutes, and developing their small resources, by means of hiring out their lands and encouraging agriculture, and no further mention is made of the supervision of the officious Bishops of Montefeltro.

A curious document, luckily preserved in the archives of San Marino, reveals the notions with which these early republicans regarded their liberty, expressing sentiments which are by no means fully realised centuries later amongst the most inveterate republicans. It runs as follows:—'When Ranieri, the abbot of St. Anastasia, was employed by Boniface VIII. to look into the state of affairs on Mount Titanus, he enquired of the citizens what they meant by their "*liberty*," and was answered thus, "Because the men belong to themselves, because they owe no homage to anyone amongst themselves, but only to the Master of all things." '

Nevertheless, the Sammarinesi did not live thus without many difficulties from without, for

the Popes, from their exile at Avignon, sent
legates to look after their Italian provinces, who
filled the pages of Italian history with many a
scene of oppression.

Hildebrand, Bishop of Arezzo, was appointed
rector of Romagna, and one Teodorico occupied
the post of canon of St. Leo under him. This
worthy canon thought himself entitled to certain
dues from San Marino, which the republicans
refused to pay, thereupon Teodorico repaired to
Rimini, and consulted a skilled lawyer, Palamede by name, giving him instructions to look
carefully into the case. Palamede did so, and
in his award declared our Republic to be free
from all external influence. This was a cause
of great gladness to the free-born mountaineers,
who have henceforth held the name of Palamede in great respect, and to this day it is a
favourite one to bestow on young republicans.
This award was again of service to them in
1296, when the case of some tribute due to
Boniface VIII. was disputed, and decided in
favour of the Sammarinesi by the above-mentioned Ranieri, abbot of St. Anastasia.

As prosperity increased under the kindly atmosphere of liberty, many envious eyes were cast up towards Mount Titanus, and the following curious story furnishes us with a good instance of the clerical rapacity of the day.

SAN MARINO FROM RIMINI HARBOUR.

Benvenuto was Bishop of Montefeltro for many years at the beginning of the fourteenth century ; with fraudulent intent he went to the Malatesti at Rimini, and represented to them that he was entitled to certain dues and tribute

from San Marino, but that by reason of the
assistance given to the republicans by the hostile
house of Feltria he was unable to enforce them
himself. However, he agreed to make over
these rights for a handsome sum of money to
the Lords of Rimini, who might be better able
to maintain them.

At this time John XXII. was the representative of St. Peter, and held his court at
Avignon, and by means of his legate Almerico
in Romagna, he countenanced the attempt of
Benvenuto, inasmuch as thereby he hoped to
strike another blow at the Counts of Urbino, by
depriving them of their firm ally. Before rati-
fying this contract the Lords of Rimini called
in the assistance of an advocate, and all was
done in proper form. But the most astounding
fact of all is that it was never carried out ; in
the annals of Rimini no mention was ever made
of possession being taken of any rights and dues
of San Marino, and furthermore, a few years
later, when the Feltrian house was banished
from Urbino, and unable in any way to assist
the Republic, we find the men of San Marino

entering into a treaty with the Malatesti for
mutual protection. And finally, as a crowning
point to the complication of the story, Benvenuto himself when chased away from his see at
San Leo, came as a fugitive, and was kindly
received at San Marino. The real solution of
this episode must be looked for at Avignon,
where the extraordinary character of John
XXII. will easily account for any eccentricity
in diplomacy in which the Pontiff was in any
way concerned. Whether money really passed
between the Malatesti and Benvenuto does not
transpire ; probably if it did, it eventually found
its way to the coffers of Avignon. 'John
XXII. was the most insatiate of pontiffs,' says
Fleury, and his treasure was put down by Vil-
lani at twenty-five millions of florins. In short,
the Popes at Avignon furnish us with examples
of excesses in everything; for whilst John
XXII. busied himself in inventing the system
of ' *annates*' and other extortions, the licen-
tiousness of the court of Clement VII. shocked
even that immoral age.

Let us now take a glance at the condition of

the House of Feltria. During the lifetime of
Count Guido the domain was being constantly
extended. Urbino had been won by the arms
of Buonconte, and with it the family was invested
by the Pope with the title of Count of Urbino,
which superseded the name of Montefeltro.
Cagli and Gubbio were soon added to their
jurisdiction, and subsequently by marriages
their territories were increased. On the death
of Guido the family went through a period of
misfortune, owing to their adherence to the
Ghibelline cause. Federigo, who succeeded his
father, was murdered together with his son,
and the family was banished from the patrimony
by the inhabitants, who put themselves under
the immediate jurisdiction of the Holy See.
But owing to the extortions and bad government of the Papal Deputies, they at length recognised their mistake, and summoned another
son of Federigo, the Count Nolfo, to rule over
them. The first years after his restoration were
disturbed by the revolt of his uncle Speranza,
who attempted to establish himself as the head
of the family, but his efforts were crushed, and

we shortly find him adding to the list of fugitives who found a harbour of refuge on Mount Titanus.

In Italy generally the affairs were rapidly approaching that state of anarchy which resulted from the establishment of the system of hiring warfare, and of the Free Companies, which demoralised the very foundation of society, whilst the Popes were at Avignon with no real power in their Italian states, and whilst the Empire was divided amongst itself, so as to allow of its exercising no influence abroad. Hence there was every opportunity for the development of individualism, and the establishment of separate interests all over the peninsula. Safe in her Lagunes, Venice had for some time past ruled in the Adriatic, whilst Genoa aimed at a corresponding position on the other coast. In Florence, Siena, and Perugia, strong republics were established, which rivalled and even surpassed in riches many of the sovereigns in Europe, whilst others of smaller importance were dotted all over Tuscany. It was owing to this rise of individuality that the system of hiring

mercenary troops gained such ground in Italy,
so detrimental to her prosperity as a nation.
Florence and Genoa first started the idea in the
thirteenth century, and from the force of circumstances all other States were obliged to follow
this example. But it was not till after the ex-
peditions of the Emperor Henry VII. in 1310,
and Louis of Bavaria in 1326, and John, King
of Bohemia, in 1331, that a sufficient nucleus
of straggling Germans was found to form the
' Great Company,' as it was called, under Duke
Guarnieri, or Werner. The French wars
of Edward III. being completed, numerous
warriors found themselves out of employment,
and hearing of the richness of Italy, and the
good opportunities afforded them of turning an
honest penny, they flocked in crowds to fight
the battles of those whose money was the only
thing they did not despise. Sir John Hawkwood
formed the natural leader of his countrymen,
who, after many vicissitudes, finally settled
down as a faithful *employé* of Florence, and his
tomb is now seen in the cathedral of that city,
erected by the grateful citizens to the memory

of Giovanni Acuto, as he was called in Italy. This period is one in which the foreign element was entirely predominant in Italian warfare; but the native martial spirit was not altogether dead, and towards the close of the fourteenth century we find the mountains of Romagna and the plains of Lombardy producing a race of warriors who entirely superseded the northern adventurers, and made the system of mercenary warfare in Italy purely Italian.

Meanwhile in Rome, during the absence of the Pontiffs, we find strange outbursts of smouldering liberty, at the head of which Cola di Rienzi stands out as a name well known to everyone; no one is ignorant of how he established his ephemeral Republic, or of how eventually he was incarcerated by the Pontiffs themselves, and all the wild enthusiasm of the hour was crushed never again to revive.

But the Popes at Avignon learnt a lesson from this, that their Italian property must be more closely looked after, or else it would slip for ever from their grasp. With this view, Innocent VI., one of the most politic of the

Avignon Popes, selected Cardinal Albornoz, the Spanish Bishop of Toledo, as a fitting person to repair to Italy with full power to reinstate the Papal authority. Knowing the hold that Rienzi had over the popular mind, his first step was to release the demagogue from his prison, and use him as a tool to win over the people to the Papal side. Fra Moreale, a celebrated *condottiere*, was, through Rienzi's instrumentality, induced to join the standard of Albornoz, and thus armed the Cardinal proceeded to reduce the Pope's refractory vassals one by one. After strenuous exertions, the whole of Romagna was made subservient to the Papacy. To illustrate the part San Marino played throughout this invasion, we will quote the words of Ugolini, the Italian historian of the Dukes of Urbino: 'The Cardinal having reduced all the Feltrian province to the Church, wondered how a place so weak as San Marino should dare to resist him. This Titanic rock was a beam in his eye. At first he excommunicated some of the citizens for opposing the direct sovereignty of the Church, and then, by the intervention of the Counts of

Urbino, the excommunication was suspended ;
nevertheless, he continued to trouble these
mountaineers, so zealous of their freedom. The
surpassing power of the Legate caused them no
little anxiety, for, according to the opinion of
the times, " what the clergy take, they rarely
relinquish." But the prelate did not push his
pretentions to the extremity, and the Sammarinesi remained safe.' Again, we can but put
down the security of San Marino to the utter
insignificance in which this isolated rock was
held, rather than the clemency of Albornoz ; for
the Cardinal had to turn his attention to the
south before the conquest of Romagna was
complete, and also he must have feared that, if
too hardly pressed, the Sammarinesi would have
put themselves under the protection of the
Malatesti, who were not yet reduced to order.
The name of Albornoz is still held in detestation
in these mountains, and at San Marino is coupled
with that of Alberoni, whose machinations
against their freedom we shall see three centuries
later.[1] Albornoz shares with the Cardinal Robert

---

[1] *Vide* chapter ix.

of Geneva the credit of having perpetrated the
horrible siege of Cesena, where the women and
children were all ruthlessly slaughtered ; and in
1356, on the capitulation of Rome, the only
favour the conquered city demanded was that
the hated Cardinal should not be admitted.

From a treaty in 1356, between the Holy
See and Count Nolfo (who was kindly permitted
to remain in possession of his territories on entire subserviency), we find a clause excepting
the land or commune of San Marino from these
concessions, and likewise stating that, if the
Malatesti should be reduced to subservience,
the commune of San Marino and the protection
of the same should return to its former state.
In spite, however, of this narrow escape from
loss of liberty, we find the men of San Marino
obliged ten years later to take up arms against
their friends the Feltrians, and to assist the army
of Albornoz at the siege of San Leo, the loss of
which completed the ruin of this family. Their
feelings in this case must have been much akin
to servitude; and it is a stumbling-block in their
course of perpetual liberty, which it is hard to

put aside with such complacency, as a thing of nought, like their eulogistic historian Delfico has done.

When eventually the Popes determined to return to their natural capital in 1367, and Urban V. landed in Italy, he found the Cardinal Albornoz awaiting his arrival and Italy in a measure reduced by the force of arms; the Cardinal's days were, however, numbered, and the ceremony of the Pope's public entry into the Eternal City was damped by the death of the principal agent who had brought it about.

Beyond another legal struggle with the Bishop of Montefeltro, Peruzzi by name, when the Cardinal Adruino had succeeded Albornoz as Legate of Romagna, the Sammarinesi had no further cause for anxiety; and out of this they came victorious, and the Bishop Peruzzi appeared in person in the parish church of San Marino to promise that his relations for the future with the Republic should always be of the most friendly character. But not trusting to empty words, the inhabitants got Franceschino, a judge from

Rimini, to draw up a 'Privilegium' for ever attesting their liberty.

When Cardinal Anglico, the brother of Urban VI., and legate of Gregory XI., came to Romagna, he found the republicans in full exercise of their jurisdiction. Gregory XI. was a Pope who dearly loved statistics, and employed all his officials in collecting every fact concerning the administration of justice, population, &c., of places under his control. Thus the Cardinal Anglico, a benevolent, well-meaning man, was despatched to fill his note-book in Romagna, and the following is an extract from it:—
' The castle of San Marino, which is in the mountains in sight of Rimini, is very elevated and strong, and inaccessible. Here there are two forts, and the approach to them and the said mountain is most difficult. There are about three hundred hearths. They do not admit the power of the Church, nor anyone exercising jurisdiction in its name; they govern themselves, and pass sentence in all civil and criminal cases without any authority, *by a certain tolerance of the Church.*'

But he adds they attend at the Montefeltrian parliaments, and serve in the cavalry, and
pay a hearth-tax for the privilege of the advice
of such parliament. This, then, is a substantial evidence to the comparative independence
of San Marino, at a time when their great
supporter, the House of Feltria, was at its
weakest, and the exorbitance of the pontiff's
was at its height.

An inhabitant of Mount Titanus, who tried
in 1375 to deliver his native town over to
Claro, Bishop of Montefeltro, met with his just
reward on the gibbet. This is one of the
few instances of treachery practised by these
mountaineers amongst themselves, and, therefore, appears doubly heinous to them.

About this time the schism in the Church
of Rome, and the unsettled state of the Papal
dominions, enabled the House of Feltria to return to some of their possessions, of which
Albornoz had deprived them ; and after the
entrance of Antonio di Montefeltro into his
ancestral property, we find them in constant
hostility with Carlo Malatesta, one of the most

famous *condottieri* of the time, a warfare which
the descendants of each inherited, and which
continued between the two houses for nearly
a century, until the final overthrow of the
Malatesta family.

Meanwhile, in the disturbed state of Italy,
the mercenary generals of the age were reaping a rich harvest. Out of the foreign school
of warriors sprang many Italians who, nurtured in the arts of war, were able to carve out
for themselves handsome principalities. Alberico
da Barbiano was one of the first of these purely
Italian *condottieri*, and the company of St. George,
founded by him, was one of the most esteemed
in Italy for prowess in war, and when under
the control of the Cardinal Robert of Geneva,
afterwards Pope Clement VIII., perpetrated
some of the most horrible deeds of cruelty on
record. Out of this school sprang some men
of more lasting fame. Sforza Atendola, a common Milanese workman, was led by an omen
to embrace the profession of arms ; he became
one of the leading generals of the age, and by
receiving the gift of the march of Ancona from

the Pope, he found himself raised to the rank
of princes. He afterwards married the heiress
of the Visconti, and by force of arms, backed
up by marital pretensions, possessed himself of
the Duchy of Milan. Braccio da Montone, a
citizen of Perugia, not unfrequently caused our
Republic to tremble by his proximity ; he was
for many years a rival of Sforza in the arts of
war, and became a potent prince in his native
town. But it was with Carlo Malatesta that
San Marino was most closely brought into connection. This prince consolidated greatly the
power of his house ; like many of his race he
took the heroes of antiquity for his model, and
aimed at virtues which he did not possess ; he
was the most diplomatic of these *condottieri*,
and consequently possessed a reputation more
extensive than his power.

The complications which arose around our
Republic out of this system of warfare, and the
final triumph of the House of Feltria, we will
allude to in the next chapter.

CHAPTER VI.

COMMENCEMENT OF THE GOLDEN ERA IN THE UMBRIAN MOUNTAINS.

Je suis monarchiste en France, et républicain à St. Marin.—
CHATEAUBRIAND.

THE close of the fourteenth century and the incoming of the next is celebrated in European history for the great schism in the Church; and as the history of Romagna, and consequently, that of San Marino, was materially affected by the events which shook Roman Catholicism to its foundation, and opened a new line of thought not only to Italy, but to the whole of Christendom, we must give a short sketch of the events as they stand.

No sooner had the intimidated cardinals in conclave in Rome been forced into electing an Italian Pontiff in the shape of Urban VI., than they repented them of their folly in being thus

coerced, and fled to Anagni, from whence they
imposed on the world the Cardinal Robert of
Geneva (the ruthless *condottiere*, who led the
Breton Free Companies) as a rival Pontiff, under
the name of Clement VIII. Thus all Europe was
divided in its adherence, and scope was given
for party spirit under the cover of religion.
Italy adhered to its native Pontiff, whilst Clement found a harbour of refuge in Avignon.

These rival Popes chiefly amused themselves with anathematising each other, and sup-
porting rival claimants for the crown of Naples.
This distracted country, by means of the will
of Joanna I., was bequeathed as a legacy to
Louis of Anjou, nephew of the king of France,
and hence formed an excellent object for the
centre of rival interests ; and to support the
cause of Ladislaus, Pope Boniface IX., successor
in Italy to Urban VI., scrupled not to extort
money by every means in his power from his
adherents. A good instance of this Pontiff's
avarice is afforded us by his conduct towards
San Marino. Again, a Bishop of Montefeltro
appears on the scene to proffer his claims, now

almost proverbial, over Mount Titanus, and
again the pontifical arm was sought in support
thereof. The avaricious Boniface, however,
granted the bishop permission to pursue his
claims, solely on condition that a large share of
the profits should find their way into the Papal
coffers. But from the fact that nothing further
is heard of the bishop's schemes, we may argue
that the trouble in executing his project would
hardly have compensated him, when he had to
share the greater part of his spoils with so
grasping a superior.

The great distress in Rome, when Ladislaus
repaid his supporters by trying to add to his
dominion the Eternal City itself, and the empti-
ness of the pontifical coffers, assisted greatly
to the re-establishment of the Feltrian House
in Urbino. Town after town exchanged their
allegiance from the Pope to the Montefeltri,
and as, of all the provinces of Italy, Romagna
possessed the most warlike inhabitants, in fact,
the sole nucleus of native spirit, the Popes in
their embarrassment were unable to offer any
resistance.

About this time an aged Venetian, Angelo
Corario by name, succeeded Boniface in his restricted pontifical honours as Gregory XII.,
whilst France continued to be the mainstay of
the Avignon Pope Benedict XIII. Thus it
was when the Council of Pisa, gathered together to heal this schism, presented the Catholic
world with a third Pope, instead of assuaging
the difficulty. John XXIII. was a man of great
spirit, and a fine specimen of the warlike bishop
of the age. Before he advanced on Rome, Pope
Gregory fled towards his native lagunes, and
passing by Rimini, sought the protection of
the inhabitants of Mount Titanus. The open-
hearted republicans were thus placed in a position of great difficulty—desirous of affording a
halting-place to the aged fugitive, but at the
same time recognising the dangers they would
thereby incur. In their extremity they sought
the advice of Count Guidantonio di Monte-
feltrio, who sagely advised the republicans to
close their gates to the fugitive Pope. Gregory, thus abandoned, was constrained to throw
himself on the protection of his native country,

and from a comparative obscurity there he continued to annoy the world by his persistency in
adhering to his pontifical honours, from which
death alone could separate him.

Meanwhile, in Germany, the Empire was
gaining strength, and in the person of Sigismond we again hear of imperial influence on Italian soil. He it was who induced John XXIII.
to consent to a Grand Council of the Church,
and he it was who finally caused this Council
to be assembled at Constance. Here Pope John
was deposed, and here another was raised in his
stead to the chair of St. Peter, without any of
those reforms being carried out for which purpose the Council had been nominally assembled.
Then the Christian world saw Martin V. in full
pontifical power, able to deal with each nation as
he chose, and the old hold on men's minds again
restored, not a whit shaken by the long schism,
since the spirit of reform was not yet strong
enough to declare itself. But as a temporal power
the Papacy was not as it had been, with empty
coffers, and society rotten in the very heart of
its dominions. Hence the Popes could do but

H

little to restore their lost supremacy in Romagna, for which favoured spot in Italy two
centuries of prosperity were in store.

The House of Feltria commenced, as it were,
a new lease of greatness with Antonio in 1376:
though owing a certain allegiance to the Popes,
the bond of union became less and less, and as
they grew more and more liberal-minded with
each successive Count, the hold they had on the
people after a hundred years of this re-establishment was greater and more substantial than
that of any other Italian potentate. They not
only occupied themselves in arms, leading their
brave mountaineers to constant victories, and
returning to their capital with well-laden purses,
with which to beautify the towns and mitigate
the taxes of their people, but also they shone
brilliantly in the world of art. The Count
Antonio himself wrote sonnets, savouring certainly more of religion than of poetry, whilst
his daughter Battista was one of the most
talented ladies of the age; married early in life
to Galeazzo Malatesta, of Pesaro, she was not
long before she tasted domestic troubles; her

husband left her, and then she devoted herself
entirely to a contemplative life, writing on
human frailty, and the true faith ; in 1433 she
gave a Latin harangue to the Emperor Sigismond on his visit to Italy, and finally took
the veil as a follower of St. Francis. The next
count, Guidantonio, was an able warrior, and
added Gubbio to his territories, became grand
constable of Ladislaus, King of Naples, and
eventually, when he came to terms with John
XXIII., he received the title of Gonfaloniere of
the Church, and Vice-General of Romagna. In
his war with Braccio da Montone, the celebrated Perugian condottiere, San Marino was
placed in difficulties ; Carlo Malatesta was most
importunate in pressing the Republic into his
service against the victorious Papal arms, but
by some means, which do not transpire, the Republic managed to maintain its neutrality ; and
when, eventually, Florence patched up a peace
between the contending parties, we find each
side loading the little Republic with favours.
Martin V. admitted their exclusive right to
elect their own justices of appeal ; Guidantonio

exempted them from paying taxes on the lands
held by republicans in the Count's territories,
whilst Sigismondo Pandolfo Malatesta, in
consideration of losses the Republic had sus-
tained in the late wars, followed Guidantonio's
example.

About this time a daughter of the House of
Montefeltro married a son of the lord of Rimini's,
and in the mountains of the Romagna everything seemed to augur peace and prosperity for
the future.   The republicans were present at
these nuptials, bringing with them a gift for the
happy pair.

But this cloudless horizon was soon to be
darkened by the insidious cunning of Sigismondo Pandolfo on the one hand, and by the
short but disastrous reign of Oddantonio di
Montefeltro on the other.

The life of this young Count Oddantonio,
who was made Duke of Urbino by Eugenius IV.,
is shrouded in mystery. Certain it is that when
he was left at the head of affairs, still quite
young, he was surrounded by evil advisers, and
gave himself up to a course of dissipation, which

alienated the affections of his subjects, and brought him to an untimely end at the hand of an assassin, and with him became extinct the last legitimate heir of the noble House of Feltria.

But in those days the question of legitimacy was one of minor importance : for example, in the House of Malatesta two illegitimate sons succeeded in succession to the lordship of Rimini. In the annals of Naples, Milan, and other Italian states, we find that the bar-sinister was of slight import, provided the claim were well backed up by force of arms.

Thus in Urbino we find Federigo, the illegitimate son of Guidantonio, taking the possessions of his ancestors without a murmur. So popular and high-minded was he that his accession was hailed with delight, and his reign, which continued till 1482, forms one of the most brilliant episodes in Italian history of that day.

A comparison between Federigo and Sigismondo Pandolfo will afford us examples of two distinct classes of Italian potentates, and as their

history for the next twenty years is most inti-
mately connected with that of our Republic, let
us here, for a moment, look into the characters
of these two remarkable men.   About the only
point they had in common was a love of art,
but what different tastes they displayed in the
pursuit of it is exemplified to-day by the contrast between Rimini and Urbino, the capitals
they respectively beautified.

Sigismondo, intensely eccentric, and intensely idealistic, erected a temple to himself
and his paramour Isotta, savouring much of the
pagan style.   This he covered, outside and in,
with the monogram which is everlastingly com-
memorative of his immoral life, whilst his three
wives, successively murdered, are honoured in
no way, except in name.   This temple, as it is
still termed, is like the illicit offspring of some
heated brain; the architect, Alberti, was partially
mad, and its founder was partially inhuman,
both the forerunners of that Renaissance school
which delighted in covering the hoary objects
of antiquity with fantastic devices.   Urbino,
on the other hand, affords us an example

of all that is delicate and refined. In the
stately palace which crowns the town every
detail is exquisite, and from the lovely stone
carvings, which adorn each door and chimney-
piece, to the intricate intarsia work on the walls,
every stone, and every conception, marks the
exquisite refinement of the Court where the

COIN OF FEDERIGO D'URBINO.

artist, the poet, and the philosopher found a
sanctuary and a home. It is a characteristic of
the House of Malatesta that they more or less
worshipped the philosophers of antiquity, whilst
it is equally characteristic of the House of Montefeltro that so many of them assumed the cowl
of St. Francis, in which to end their days.

No better example of Sigismondo's duplicity

can be anywhere found than in his constant
insidious attempts to possess himself of the castle
of San Marino. From the frequent instances on
record, the desire of getting so strong a vantage
ground against his enemies must have been continually on his mind—a restless, troubled mind,
always suspicious of his friends, and always
trying to overreach his foes.

The constant dread he felt lest Mount Titanus
should become a centre of attack against him is
quaintly illustrated by a legendary story attached
to the monastery of Valdragone, situated in a wild
spot amongst some tufous refts outside the Borgo.
It runs as follows : In the thirteenth century a
pious man left in the Republic's charge a sum of
money with which to found a monastery of the
order of Servites on this weird spot. Nevertheless, from causes unknown, this bequest was
never carried out. As years rolled on, numerous
tales of horror were told of a fierce dragon
which appeared on the spot, so terrifying the
peasants that the place was called *Valdragone*,
which it retains to this day. The republicans,
however, were unable to appease this monster,

owing to the lack of money in their coffers;
doubtless the legacy had long since found its
way into some other channel, when one day
there arrived from Siena a man who called
himself Spanocchi, alleging that he had come,
under Divine inspiration, to build the monastery
in question. The republicans gladly received
him, and with their accustomed hospitality
pressed him to come the following year. This
he did, and again presented himself not empty-
handed, for he brought his friends a picture
painted in oils, and representing the Madonna
and Child supported by the virgin saints Bar-
bara and Catharine, and so wonderful were
the miracles wrought by this that the credulous
flocked from all parts to worship and behold.

Meanwhile the crafty Sigismondo looked
askance on the concourse of people on the
dangerous heights of Mount Titanus, recognising
in this the centre of some deep-laid plot. He
forbad any of his subjects to repair to the holy
spot, and sent assassins under cover of night to
seize the pious Spanocchi, and bring him to
Rimini. The tyrant's ruffians found no difficulty

in possessing themselves of their prey ; but, lo ! after walking with him all night, as they thought in the direction of Rimini, they were electrified at break of day to find themselves still by the cross, which Spanocchi had erected as an object of reverence for the numerous pilgrims. Fearing to return without executing in some way their master's wishes, they hurriedly gibbeted Spanocchi on his own cross, and made off home with all speed. No sooner were they out of sight, than the rope broke, and Spanocchi fell down quite safely. He was soon surrounded by crowds of the admiring republicans, and became more than ever an object of veneration ; but, having thus so narrowly escaped, he wisely decided not again to tempt Providence, being in no way ambitious of a martyr's crown. He was obdurate to the entreaties of the Sammarinesi ; he left the Republic without delay, never to return. But he left his works behind him ; the dragon was seen no more ; and the little monastery still exists, where a few monks drag on their weary hours and drink their sparkling wine regardless of the world around them.

Meanwhile Federigo d'Urbino was reaping for himself those laurels which we find inscribed in large letters around the *cortile* of his own palace of Urbino. As captain-general of the forces of the King of Naples, and Gonfaloniere of the Church, he acquired enormous wealth, which he devoted to the embellishment of his cities, and to the alleviation of the poverty of his subjects. He assisted the Sammarinesi in re-building and extending their wall, and, as all writers attest, he treated our little Republic with true fatherly feeling, not entirely without self-interest, perhaps, as in his wars against Sigismondo Mount Titanus formed an excellent *pièce de résistance.* Being himself well up in letters, Federigo spent much time and trouble in collecting books, and formed that celebrated library of Urbino which now forms the nucleus of the Vatican collection; in fact, in the words of Tasso, he ushered in that era in Urbino which made it 'the stay and refuge of gifted men.' In later years he received the Order of the Garter from the English Edward IV., which is now seen represented on the roof of his private studio, conspicuous amongst his other orders.

Let us now take a glance at the Papacy, which is to play an important part in the events to follow. The age of Councils was now at its height. Pressed by the Emperor on one side and popular feeling on the other, the Popes could do nothing but try to bias the current of feeling, and arrange that these Councils should be held in a place where their influence was greatest.

Eugenius IV., with this intent, opposed to the utmost the Council held in Basle, but it was in vain that he busied himself at Ferrara with trying to amalgamate the Eastern and the Western Church, and it was in vain that he threw obstacles in the way of this Teuton Council. He found himself deposed by a power stronger than his own.

Thus, after two Pontiffs of slight political importance had occupied the chair of St. Peter, of whom Nicholas V. tended more to develope the rising spirit of art than to consolidate the Papal power, the great mover in the Council of

Basle, Æneas Sylvius Piccolomini, found himself raised to the Pontificate under the name of Pius II. This man, a native of Siena, had passed through the phases of Secretary to a Pope, an Emperor, and a Council, hence we could hardly imagine anyone better calculated to govern the politics of the age. By his skill the Papacy was restored to its original footing, and freed from external thraldom. After his day we find the vices of a Pontiff's career in no way controlled. Yet the pontificate of Pius II. did not form a precedent for the school he initiated. Old and feeble, he abandoned his former vigour of policy, and one project alone occupied his mind, that of a crusade, and this was only diverted by the conduct of Sigismondo Pandolfo. From his strongholds around Rimini he continued to harass his neighbours with restless infidelity. Federigo d'Urbino and Sigismondo had been the pupils of rival condottieri. They had challenged each other to single combat, and the germs of rivalry thus begun continued when they were established in their respective domains. A day of satisfaction, however, was in store for all enemies of the

House of Malatesta. Alfonso, King of Aragon, had been cheated out of some money by the crafty Sigismondo. The Pope was enraged on account of his lawless disrespect of his feudal superior. Federigo d'Urbino, as captain-general of the one, and as gonfaloniere of the other, was nothing loath to join in an alliance against his hereditary foe.

San Marino, thus placed, had no other course to pursue but to throw in its lot with this overwhelming league, and thereby, as we shall see, reaped no small advantage.

CHAPTER VII.

CONTINUED PROSPERITY.

A prince's greatest stronghold is his people's love.
MACHIAVELLI, *Il Principe.*

IN the year 1453 great consternation was felt
throughout Christendom at the fall of Con-
stantinople, and the threatening aspect of the
Turks. Nowhere was there greater cause for
alarm than on the eastern coast of Italy, for
from the towers of San Marco at Venice the
smouldering fires of the Ottoman devastators
were visible.

It was with the intention of organising a
crusade against these invaders that Pius II.
summoned his Council at Mantua; but the
ardour for crusades was gone, and party spirit
in Italy ran too high to allow any potentate
to think of quitting his own territories for a
precarious warfare in the East.

Thus Federigo d'Urbino, who was to have been captain-general of this expedition, at the very time of the sitting of the Council, was busily engaged, with the assistance of the condottiere Piccinino, in reducing Sigismondo Pandolfo to order. And, perhaps, all that Pius II. can be said to have achieved by his presence in this part of Italy was the humble submission of the restless Malatesta, who, hedged in on all sides, was obliged to give way to the force of circumstances, and appear in submission at the Council of Mantua. In fact, the Pope hesitated, until necessary, to drive Sigismondo to extremities, fearing that he might be led to call in Turkish aid before he could be reduced to order.

No one, however, was readier to shake off the cloak of humility when circumstances were favourable than Sigismondo. By a dexterous application of his wiles, he won over the condottiere Piccinino to his side, and the following year we learn, from letters addressed by Federigo d'Urbino to the Sammarinesi, that danger was again imminent from the side of Rimini, and that they had better prepare for war. At this time an exceeding wise man, Calcigni by name, was the Solon on Mount Titanus. Long and weighty were his arguments to warn his countrymen from running headlong into war. But the Council of Twelve, assembled to consider the point, eventually decided that Calcigni's wisdom was of that character which rejoices in doing nothing; hence the sage's words were unheeded, and San Marino, yielding to the persuasions of Federigo, joined the alliance between the Pope, the King of Naples, and the Duke of Urbino, against the House of Malatesta, and thus, almost for the first and last time, do we find our little Republic fairly launched into a war on its own account. The war was of short duration, for the Lord of Rimini was unable for long to hold out against such odds. Pius thundered his excommunications against him, whilst Federigo pressed him hard up to the very walls of Rimini. And in 1463 the once stately lord of numerous castles and towns in Romagna was obliged to relinquish all his territories, save Rimini and five miles around it, with a reversion

on his death of even this to the Papal See,
whilst the same sentence was passed on his
brother, Domenico, Lord of Cesena.

In dividing the spoils of victory the King of
Naples was satisfied with the original debt and
his expenses paid ; the Pope got 1,000 gold
ducats and a handsome list of towns to add to
the Papal dominions ; Federigo d'Urbino thereby won Pesaro and the coast line almost up to
the gates of Rimini, together with Verruchio
and the boundary line of the Marrechia, whilst
our little Republic was by no means neglected
in the distribution of spoil. The township of
Serravalle, containing a castle and several noble
families, likewise the hamlets of Fiorentino,
Mongiardino, and Faetano, were placed under
the government of San Marino. ' By a great
kindness of the Pope,' sneers Carlo Fea, was
this done ; but if it was kindness alone to requite the assistance of an ally, at least the fact
stands as it is, that these few villages were
handed over to the Republic, and thereby its
capacity for self-government was indisputably
recognised for ever.

This, perhaps, forms the most brilliant era
in the lifetime of our little community, a
brilliancy which, luckily for itself, did not further expand. Its prosperity could go thus far,
and no farther, without exciting the cupidity of
its more powerful neighbours. A further advantage accrued to San Marino out of this war :
it henceforth no longer styled itself a 'community,' but a '*republic*,' and was recognised as
such through the length and breadth of Italy,
from Naples to the haughty Venice. The well-
known historian of this latter country, Pietro
Bembo, speaks of San Marino about this time
as 'an exceeding high mountain, which ad-
ministers itself as a republic, and obeys no
king.' [1]

Pius II. did not, however, relinquish his plan
of a crusade with this. An armament was
prepared at Ancona, whither the Pope repaired
to give it a parting blessing ; but death snatched
him away on the eve of realising his day-dream,
and with him expired all desire to arouse
Christendom in its own defence. It was Venice

[1] Bembo, *Storia Veneta.*

which was to be the great bulwark of Europe
against the Ottoman encroachments, and under
the banner of San Marco the restless spirit of
Sigismondo Pandolfo found the occupation it
loved, until old age compelled him to return to
Rimini, to die on the stage of his former greatness   Assisted by a league between Naples,
Florence, and Urbino, his illegitimate son, Ro-
berto Malatesta, managed to maintain himself as
Lord of Rimini against the claims of Paul II.
But he was essentially a man of peace, and
henceforth we hear no more of subtle plans on
the side of Rimini for enslaving the inhabitants
of Mount Titanus.

The even tenor of the next few years is
solely broken by some marriage festivities
amongst Federigo's goodly array of daughters,
at which the men of San Marino were always
present in their best attire, bringing with them
a propitiatory offering.

Out of one of these marriages sprang events
of importance for Romagna, for Federigo had
but one son, Guidobaldo, a delicate youth,
who, though he reigned for many years after

his father, left no offspring, and hence the duchy would have lapsed to the Holy See, had not Federigo's daughter, Giovanna, married Giovanni della Rovere, nephew of Sixtus IV., and brother of Julius II., and hence this latter Pontiff was content to see his nephew succeed as heir to the noble House of Feltria ; but before this event other and graver affairs were to break the serenity which had reigned so long in the Umbrian Mountains.

It had been the object of most of the leading rulers in Italy to maintain this peace. Ferdinand in Naples, Ludovico Sforza in Milan, and Lorenzo de' Medici in Florence, were together desirous of rest ; hence by their unity they could keep in check the encroachments of Venice, and procure that peace which Italy so much required.

During this period Federigo d'Urbino breathed his last, stricken by the plague at Ferrara in 1482, deeply lamented by everyone, and by none more than by the inhabitants of Mount Titanus. His affability and generosity in his own dominions preserved his long reign of nearly forty years from a single insurrection. From his stately palace he used daily to descend into the market-place, and chat with his subjects on equal terms. In fact, his whole career is an anomaly in those times, considering the school in which he had been trained, and the examples he saw around him. His son and successor, Guidobaldo I., continued the same policy, but without his father's strength of character. Towards San Marino he was always kind and indulgent; but his lot was cast in the troubled times of the Borgias, when all the centre of Italy was disturbed by the wiles of Alexander VI. and his son.

Cæsar Borgia's occupation of Romagna and his ephemeral reign on Mount Titanus form the next episode in our history.

No characters of the middle ages have afforded more food for commentary and more food for scandal than the history of the Borgian family. No character has ever been maligned more than that of Lucrezia's, though, thanks to the efforts of Gregorovius, much of the foul guilt attached to her name has been washed

away. But no one has ever attempted in any
way to extenuate the deeds of Alexander and
his son. Bathed in the lowest depths of villany
and vice, they are names of execration amongst
their countrymen even now. ' The father never
did what he said, and the son never said what
he did,' is an Italian saying full of force, which
well describes them. Of the tales of treachery
in connection with their history, that of the
capture of Urbino is but one of the mildest, yet
serving in its way to illustrate the base treachery
of their actions.

Dreams of an Italian unity in the person of
his son floated before the eyes of the hoary
Pontiff; fief after fief was heaped on the grasping head of Cesare Borgia ; and French aid was
sought to further these plans. Thus with little
difficulty most of the towns of Romagna were
reduced, and from the towers of Mount Titanus
the Papal banner was seen to float over the
towns of Rimini, Forlì, and Cesena. Prudence
had always been amongst the qualities of the
Sammarinesi, and instead of offering any resistance, they despatched men and money to swell

the forces of the usurper, hoping thus to avert their doom.

But the cunning of Borgia was shortly to be directed against Urbino. This mountain duchy formed an eyesore in his newly-acquired dukedom of Romagna, and though Guidobaldo had in every way sought to avoid a quarrel with Cesare, yet this was not to be left an obstacle in his path. Hence the following plan was adopted by the Duke Cesare and his father for reducing Urbino.

The ancient family of Varano were still lords of Camerino, and Giulio Cesare Varano, the representative of his race, had imprudently offered an asylum to the rebels of the Church. For this offence Alexander VI. deprived him of his fief, and to carry out this sentence Duke Cesare repaired with a small army to Perugia, at the same time demanding of Guidobaldo d'Urbino the use of his army to enable him to carry out his plans. Guidobaldo, afraid to compromise himself with so powerful a neighbour, sent all he could. When Cesare Borgia had thus removed all the resources of the Duke, he openly declared his intentions against Urbino. The scare that was created by this sudden invasion, and the entire surprise with which it took the Duke, who was quietly supping in the gardens of a convent near Urbino, is best related by a letter which Guidobaldo himself penned from Venice, where he was obliged to take refuge, to the Cardinal della Rovere, afterwards Julius II. : 'Supposing myself in perfect security, whilst at supper, I received several pieces of intelligence which made me hurry back to Urbino, and there I found a message from the authorities of San Marino informing me that the remaining thousand infantry of Romagna had advanced upon Verruchio and San Arcangelo, well officered, and occasioning them great alarm. Presently there reached me a letter from the Commissioner of Cagli, intimating that the Duke had avowed hostile intentions, and would reach Urbino next morning. This place being in all respects unprovided for resistance, and its defences of no strength, I thought it well to make the best of my way on horseback, together with the Lord Prefect, three faithful people, and a

few archers to San Leo, my strongest fortress
in Montefeltro, which is accessible only by two
passes.   I left instructions that matters should
be so arranged that Urbino might suffer as little
as possible, and at midnight I set out.   By dawn
I reached a castle four miles distant from San
Leo, and there learned that troops from Verruchio and San Arcangelo, instead of marching
upon San Marino, had seized the passes of San
Leo, which was surrounded on all sides by the
men of Rimini and Cesena well-armed.   On
hearing this, I despatched a person to ascertain
how things were, and took the road to Sant'
Agata, another of my Montefeltrian castles on
the confines of Tuscany and Romagna, which,
though not of great strength, was a good quarter,
and there I halted for a short rest for the horses,
then nearly dead.   Dismissing the archers, I
with three mounted followers thought it best to
separate from the Lord Prefect, who with two
of his people took the most secure road to the
Val di Bagno, whilst I, disguised as a peasant,
followed the mountain paths towards the Tuscan
frontier.   At about fourteen miles from Sant'

Agata, at a stream called the Borello, I was attacked by some country people, who pursued us with the cries of "Blood! blood!" When within a bowshot of me they seized one of my people, who carried my money, and our guide: but the rest of us, with great difficulty, reached Castel Nuovo, a small place belonging to the illustrious Signory.' Thus, after many hair-breadth escapes, Guidobaldo reached Venice, and San Leo alone held out for some time, until it, too, was treasonably surrendered, and all Romagna was at the feet of Duke Valentino. In such a position as this, San Marino had but one course to pursue to retain its freedom, and that was to throw itself on the protection of Venice, where their protector, Guidobaldo, had found a harbour of refuge. The Serene Republic, how-ever, could send them nothing but words of comfort and hope.' Thus our Republic, of ne-cessity, fell into the vortex of subjugation which the Borgias brought on this peaceful land. For in 1503 we find a book of condemnations, stating that some were 'passed by a learned

---

[1] Bembo, *Storia Veneta.*

vice-regent, one Hercules Spaveldo, acting on behalf of that most famous and excellent lord, Cesare Borgia, for the territory of San Marino.' Whilst towards the close of the same year we again read in the same book that all sentences were 'passed by the honourable captains of the liberty of San Marino.' Thus in Mount Titanus we, perhaps, see almost the last victim of the Borgias. Their trial was short, and there are no records of its having been so severe as their neighbours, and San Marino returned peaceably to its former state of government, when Cæsar's fortunes were ruined by his father's death, and when Guidobaldo returned to the throne of his ancestors.

The few years that still remained to him Guidobaldo spent in the pursuit of art, and in carrying on the works of his father. A curious echo of the times is found in the wit levelled against the Borgias after the return of Guidobaldo at the Court of Urbino. A comedy was put on the stage representing all the vices of the family, in which an essentially religious people joined heartily in the derisive representation of their spiritual chief. Surely if those so immediately under the eyes of Rome could indulge in scoffing at the Papal power, we can hardly wonder that at a distance seeds of dissension were deeply sown by their outrageous conduct.

The succeeding Pontificate of Julius II., if not so culpably immoral, at least exhibits not less openly the use made of the Papal chair to extend family interests and party feeling. Venice and her increasing power was the great bugbear of this Pontiff, and when the craven-hearted Pandolfo Malatesta, a weak scion of his house, sold his patrimony to the Serene Republic, the Pope's cup of bitterness was full. Venice also having seized many other towns in the Romagna, in the anarchy incident on the fall of the Borgias, it was thenceforth the fear of the encroaching prosperity of their sister Republic which harassed the minds of the Councillors of San Marino.

When, on the death of Guidobaldo, the last of the Montefeltri, a doubt arose as to the succession of his adopted son and nephew

Francesco Maria della Rovere, it was fortunate for Romagna and for San Marino that a pontiff of the della Rovere name held the chair of Saint Peter. For without the Church's support this family could not have held its own, Venice would have added this mountainous district to its possessions, and our small Republic would have found itself merged in the power of the greater.

All fear of this aggrandisement of Venice was set aside in 1508, when Julius II. manœuvred the league of Cambray, and foreign influence was brought to bear on the inhabitants of the lagunes, one of the last strongholds of Italian freedom. Henceforth it was existence for which Venice fought, having arrayed against her the Pope, the Kings of France and Spain, the King of the Romans, and the Dukes of Savoy and Ferrara. Our small Republic had now no further cause for alarm, and Francesco Maria found himself firmly seated on the throne of the Feltrians.

The affection in which the Sammarinesi held the last of their protecting race is shown

by their respect paid to Guidobaldo's remains.
A simple and touching picture of the times is
given in the old chronicle of this funeral, when
at the Church of San Benedetto, outside the
walls of Urbino, the last of the beloved race was
consigned to his massive marble tomb, in a spot
from whence the eye roves over the hilly fast-
nesses of Umbria, forming a background to the
towers of Urbino. To join the funeral cortége
were sent from San Marino ' eight Ambassadors,
or Deputies, all dressed in mourning, to assist
at the obsequies, and to unite their tears with
those of the good citizens of Urbino.'

With the House of Rovere a new era is
commenced, an era which, if not so brilliant as
the preceding one, was ushered in well for our
Republic, by the following letter addressed to the
captains by Francesco Maria, on his succession,
containing a promise, which we shall find was
amply fulfilled. This salutation ran as follows :—
' According to the ancient custom and example
of all the former lords of this my most illustrious
house, I think it right that I should continue to
be vigilant and prompt in executing all the good

deeds of my ancestors, and more especially in watching over your liberty, and I cannot help reminding you that no one can feel more friendly towards you than I do, though I am aware there is no occasion to do so.'

PEDIGREE OF THE HOUSE OF MONTEFELTRO.

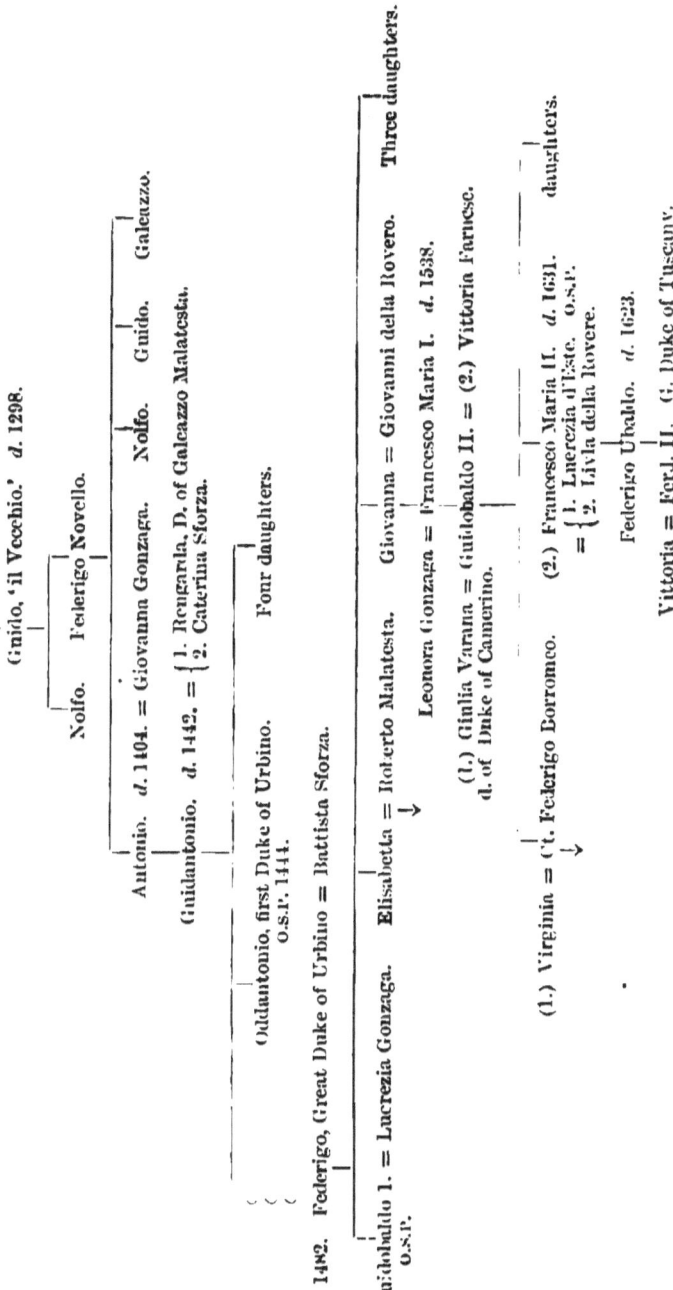

K

CHAPTER VIII.

THE STAR OF ROMAGNA BEGINS TO WANE.

BUT few of the weighty events which had occurred on the western side of the Apennines
influenced the peace of the Umbrian Mountains.
San Marino probably heard how the French
King Charles VIII. had passed through Italy
like a meteor, and then disappeared, his example forming a precedent for Louis XII., who
seized the Duchy of Milan, and for Ferdinand
of Aragon, who established himself in Naples.
With an extraordinary burst of patriotism,
Julius II. tried to free the peninsula from its
foreign scourges. After having sufficiently
humbled the Republic of Venice, he formed
the Holy League against the French ; but when
the French were gone the Spaniards were all
the stronger, and wound round the country a

coil of fetters too heavy to be broken. We
read of the perturbation and dismay with which
the Sammarinesi received their friendly but
stately Pope, when he was hurrying northward
to join his troops. Their simple habits of life
were much disconcerted by their august visitor,
but from Bologna the Pontiff addressed them a
reassuring letter, thanking them for their hospitality, extolling their liberty, and promising an
alleviation of the duties on salt, which, however, he never fulfilled, being too busily engaged in his warlike enterprises.

Difficulties, however, were again in store for
Romagna, when the House of Medici found itself omnipotent on the accession of Leo X. to the
pontificate. Forgetful of the asylum afforded
to his family by the Court of Urbino, forgetful
how Elisabetta Feltria, the pious consort of
Guidobaldo, had almost adopted his brother
Giuliano, Leo X. thought fit to set up this very
brother in the Duchy of Urbino in Francesco
Maria's stead. This worthy duke was excommunicated without cause, and ruthlessly driven
out of his dominions by the ambitious Pontiff.

With its accustomed prudence our Republic
entered into an alliance with the Medici family.
Polite letters were written to Florence, and
Lorenzo the younger interceded with his uncle
for Mount Titanus. Pieto Bembo informs us
that Leo X. was favourable to San Marino.
What did he want with this bare rock?—a
Pontiff whose sole object was to fill the papal
coffers to overflowing, to adorn his city, and to
aggrandise his family.

The satirical Ariosto has left us a good
sketch of his character in the following fable.
A shepherd once luckily discovered a deep well
in an exceedingly dry season, and had only one
small vessel with which to dispense the water
from it; firstly, he helped himself, and secondly,
his wife, and then his dear children were permitted to quench their thirst; next in turn
came such friends as had given most assistance
in digging the well; and then his cattle, taking
care to supply those first whose death would
cause him the greatest loss. At length a poor
parrot, much beloved by his master, cried out,
' Alas! I am neither one of his relatives, nor

did I assist in digging the well, nor am I likely
to be of more service to him in future than I
have been in times past.' It is needless to add,
that Leo was the shepherd, and Ariosto the
parrot, whose services were so greedily sought
for, but so poorly requited.

The siege of San Leo, which held out for
Francesco Maria, forms the most prominent
episode in this war. The Sammarinesi's coffers
were drained dry again and again to provide
money and food for the pontifical forces, and
much resembling the parrot in Ariosto's fable,
they only gained thereby a reprieval from the
excommunication under which the rest of Urbino was put, but never got any restitution of
their goods.

With the fall of San Leo the hopes of the
Duke of Urbino were nearly exhausted, but he
somehow managed to collect together a small
force, and re-entered his dominions. But who
could fight against an enemy who could raise
200,000 ducats by the sale of thirty cardinals'
hats, not to mention by other large sums from
indulgences, the origin of which is imputed to

Leo? Francesco soon found his army was corrupted, and he was obliged to flee, bidding a tender farewell to the inhabitants of Mount Titanus, as he passed northwards in his rapid flight towards Mantua, stipulating only for the transport of his artillery, and the preservation of the famous library, which Duke Federigo had collected.

It is a curious feature of these times to see all the expatriated lords hovering round their dominions, awaiting the death of a Pope. As it had been with Alexander VI., so it was with Leo X. After his decease a Malatesta is seen hurrying on the road to Rimini, a Baglione to Perugia, and Francesco Maria to Urbino. 'We are saved from the lion's claws,' jocosely said this latter, as he entered his capital, and with the lion's death his family honours relapsed to their normal condition.

The history of the next few years in Italy is that of the contest between France and Spain on Italian soil. That Francis I. was captured at Pavia was of small moment to our little State. For them it was a time of peace when the Popes were occupied in foreign complications, and no schemes of occupation hovered over their heads. The year 1530 was the date of the enslavement of Italy, when Clement VII. crowned Charles of Spain as King and Emperor. He henceforth imposed on his country an Austro-Spanish yoke, from the evil effects of which Italy has not yet recovered.

Meanwhile, in Urbino, Francesco Maria was succeeded by his son, Guidobaldo II. His spirit was not so kindly as that of his ancestors; he oppressed his people with taxes, and frequent signs of discontent showed themselves during his long reign. An eye-witness thus quaintly describes his accession, and the jealousies existing amongst his subjects :—' On the following morning there came in envoys from various places to offer their condolences, wearing mourning-robes that swept the ground. The first who were admitted to an audience were the Gonfaloniere and priors from Urbino, and then the men of San Marino. After breakfast the other communities were admitted without order, in consequence of a wrangle for precedence

between Gubbio and Pesaro, Cagli and Fossom-
brone, and this continued till seven o'clock in
the evening.'

No records of moment mention San Marino
in connection with the history of the times until
1542, when a mysterious attempt to occupy
Mount Titanus brought it prominently before
the politicians of Italy.

At this time Allessandro Farnese occupied
the chair of St. Peter as Paul III. He was a
curiously cautious man, and the first part of his
pontificate is an admirable example of cards
beautifully played between the King of France
and the Emperor Charles V., and the conse-
quent aggrandisement of his family between
the two. When the Emperor refused to shower
down any more blessings on the Pope, having
given his illegitimate daughter Margaret to the
Pope's grandson Ottaviano, with the Duchy of
Parma, Paul gradually veered round towards
the side of France, and another grandson,
Orazio, is provided with an illegitimate daughter
of Henry II. And thus armed he threw all
his weight into the Anti-Spanish faction,

opposing in every way the summoning of the Council of Trent, and even allying himself indirectly with the Protestant League of Smalkalde.

It is not to be wondered at that Paul and his family developed minor plots on their less powerful neighbours. Guidobaldo II. was deprived of the Duchy of Camerino, which was on the eve of being incorporated with Urbino; and though great indignation was expressed at this, yet the external powers were too busily engaged in their own private affairs.

Four years later, in 1542, on June 4, the roving band of Pietro Strozzi found itself at Rimini. The brothers Strozzi were Florentine exiles, and travelled about the country in the pay of the Farnese. Under cover of night this *condottiere*, with five hundred infantry and the same number of cavalry, started off on an expedition to seize San Marino. They provided themselves with scaling-ladders and implements of siege, and divided themselves into two bands, so as to take the Republic by surprise on two sides. However, as usual, the elements were in favour of San Marino; a thick mist came on, or, as some authors assert, a snowstorm ; but, judging from the season, the former is more presumable. At all events, a miracle happened, and it was attributed to the instrumentality of the Saint, who, in conjunction with S. Quirinus, on whose day it chanced to fall, threw a thick cloud round our rock ; and hence he is frequently depicted as shrouding his favourite abode with clouds, after the fashion of a hen and her chickens. Strozzi's men lost their way in the dark, so that by dawn they were far from Mount Titanus, and their plots were revealed to the inhabitants by the barking of a dog. Thus disconcerted, the invading army ran away, leaving our brave Republicans at a loss to know who their enemy had been, but thankful to their Saint and his coadjutor, whose day is still held most sacred amongst them.

Great was the compassion expressed by all potentates who were jealous of the Papal movements. Charles V. sends Señor Bustamente de Herreras to say, that it was none of his doing, and offering to take the Republic under his immediate protection. Guidobaldo of Urbino like-

wise manifests his concern, and Duke Cosmo
de Medici, of Florence, sends an embassy, offering to assist the Sammarinesi with men and
money. Thus consoled, the Republicans openly
state their suspicions that the Pope was at the
bottom of it, and this eventually proved to be
the case; they decline the Emperor's kind offer,
and ask only to be left in possession of their
government, under the immediate protection of
the Dukes of Urbino. Thus danger was again
averted, and nothing for some years occurred
to break the peace which reigned on Mount
Titanus.

About this time Guidobaldo II. wisely contracted a marriage with a niece of Paul III., and
was at peace during the remainder of his reign.
At this wedding the men from San Marino
again appear, bringing with them for a present
a large silver gilt cup, with this inscription :—
' Libertas perpetua Reipublicæ Sancti Marini.'
In short, the Republican coffers must have been
sorely taxed by the number of delicate atten-
tions they thought fit to pay to their lordly
protectors.

Meanwhile in Italy that wondrous blaze of art was filling the land with every description of beauty ; not that the story of San Marino

RAPHAEL'S STREET IN URBINO.

requires much allusion to this, yet out of compliment to the Umbrian mountains, and the Feltrian dynasty, we cannot in silence pass over the existence of Raphael and his contemporaries.

From the roof of the house where old Sanzio lived in Urbino, and where Raphael was born, the distant towers of our Republic may be descried; higher up the same steep street lived Timoteo della Vite, another great scion of the Umbrian school, whilst even San Marino itself boasts of having been the birthplace of Bramante, an architect of no mean power. Tasso was most closely connected with the Court of Urbino, and had a *casino* close to the palace of Pesaro, from whence he sang sweet strains about the Duchess, of whom scandal says he was almost too fond; nevertheless, in his ' Rinaldo ' he does ample justice to Guidobaldo's patronage, whom he thus describes :—

> He of expression stern and brow serene,
>   His mien ennobled by a royal state ;
> The great Francesco Maria's son is here,
>   In peace superior, in the field his mate ;
> Beneath whose prudent sway no peril ere
>   Urbino's favoured duchy shall await,
> While o'er her happy vales and golden plains
> A joyous and enduring summer reigns.

But we must not deprive our Republic of the one bright star which adorned it, a certain

Giovanni Battista Belluzzi, of the noble Sammarinese family of whom we hear so much.   He
was born in 1506, and studied at Pesaro under
the Gengas, being of an architectural turn of
mind ; but returning to the isolation of Mount
Titanus, he there followed his avocation of a
wool merchant, and was lost to the world until
the above-mentioned Spanish ambassador came
to San Marino after the affair of the Strozzi in
1542.   He then discovered Belluzzi's latent talents, and introduced him to Duke Cosmo of
Florence, who made him his state engineer.   To
Belluzzi the fortress of San Miniato at Florence
is due, and likewise the fortifications of Pistoja,
and his advice was the means of reducing Siena,
which had so great an influence on the politics
of the day. Belluzzi affords us a fair specimen of
San Marino's brilliant sons ; they found no scope
for their ability on their native rock, and preferred to shine at some distant court to peaceful
nonentity at home.   Doubtless his presence at
the ducal court of Florence was of advantage to
our State, for through his medium we constantly
hear of polite messages, not only from Duke

Cosmo, but also from the Emperor Charles V., to the Captains of Mount Titanus.

The exact relationship between San Marino and Guidobaldo II. is illustrated by a treaty of friendship in 1549. The Duke covenants to ' defend. protect, and guard San Marino against all persons whatsoever who may seek or wish to injure it, whether in respect to its possessions, subjects, state, or pre-eminence, holding its enemies for his enemies, and its allies for his allies, and further undertaking to accord to it all possible aid and favour in the maintenance of its independence and freedom.' The envoys of San Marino, on behalf of the Republic, covenant ' with all their exertion and power to assist, uphold, and preserve the subjects, state, honour and dignity of the said Lord Duke against whatsoever person, state, or potentate may make attempts against him, promising to hold the friends of his Excellency as their friends, and his foes as their foes, and to pay him at all times the respect due to a faithful and good protector.'

From the death of Guidobaldo, for almost

two whole centuries, the history of Italy is one
of abject slavery; the history of San Marino is
one of decadence and constitutional weakness.
Francesco Maria II., the last Duke of the Rovere
line, was constantly away, as general of Philip II.
of Spain, and though his territory enjoyed comparative peace, yet the constant drain on its
resources, and the absence of a sufficient armed
force to keep off the Saracen marauders, made
their condition pitiable in the extreme; famine
followed famine, with pestilence in its train.
But, nevertheless, the inhabitants clung with
favour to this their last Duke, and looked with
fear at the approaching extinction of the Rovere
family, for Francesco Maria had no son; however, when all hope of male offspring seemed
past, the Duchess presented him with a son, and
he was called Federigo, a fine handsome child,
who is principally known to posterity by the
picture of him by Baroccio, in gorgeous swad-
dling clothes, amongst the Pitti collection in
Florence. For this last scion of the noble house
ruined his health with early debaucheries, and
died some years before his father, whose spirits

became so broken by his trials and approaching old age, that he relinquished the reins of government in 1631, and Urbino lapsed to the Holy See during the pontificate of Urban VIII.

Beyond a slight spar with Paul IV. about a sentence the Republic had passed, and which the Pontiff professed to disapprove, no external complications occurred during the latter years of the ducal government. This was eventually settled by the intervention of the Dukes of Urbino, not before Paul had indignantly summoned the Captains before him at Rome, and the Republicans had as indignantly refused. Indeed it is truly wonderful that San Marino got off so easily from the grasp of so rigid a Pontiff, who looked at freedom as akin to heresy; but his eyes were turned north of Italy, and the small harbour of liberty was allowed to linger near home, whilst the horrors of the Inquisition and the espionage of the Jesuits elsewhere, had so far enchained men's minds as to break the spirit of even haughty Venice.

After the peace of Câteau Cambresis in 1558, the power of Philip of Spain was so

L

dominant in Italy that the merest shadow of
her former individuality was left. Amongst
free communities Venice alone continued to
be of any importance, though showing many
signs of decay, whilst Genoa and Lucca, though
nominally free, were all but in name subject to
Spain. Thus San Marino, even then, was almost
the last of its class in Italy, whilst other free
communities had been absorbed by despots and
had fallen sacrifices to party spirit, San Marino
alone continued the same, owing its preservation
to its integrity and to its nonentity in the social
scale.

When Francesco Maria felt old age coming
on, and no chance of an heir to sit on his
throne, he had prudently advised the inhabitants
of San Marino to draw up an agreement with
the Pontiff, who would henceforward be their
protector. This was postponed for some years,
on the birth of a son, as above mentioned ;
but when eventually it became necessary a
most satisfactory agreement was drawn up with
Urban VIII., a quiet well-meaning man, who
had no ambitions for extending his temporal

dominions if he had been able so to do. By
this agreement the Sammarinesi reserved their
entire liberty, as it had been in the times of the
dukes, and their entire jurisdiction, save only
and except the sovereign power of the Pope, a
sovereign power which the Pontiffs professed to
exercise over the whole of the Catholic world,
and which in no way interfered with San
Marino's exercise of its favourite liberty. In
addition to this, he gave them the right of ex-
port and import through the Papal dominions,
which had previously been subject to a tax
called ' *cinquina*.'

On this change of government not a claim
was made to appropriate the rock, and affairs
went on exactly as of yore on the summit of
Mount Titanus, save only the voice of one bishop
was raised to complain of this nest of liberty in
the heart of slavery. But as his pen was more
fluent in writing dissertations on the revelations
of St. Brigida, and other saintly lore, little heed
was given to his writings on the subject of a
Papal occupation of Mount Titanus.

Over the bridge of decadence incident on the

protectorship of the Holy See let us hurriedly
pass ; in its nature it is purely constitutional,
one scene of laxity of laws, of laxity of principle,
which must have eventually led to entire dis-
ruption of the whole frame of government. A
paucity, too, of reports, makes the period one
vast chaos, which is only relieved by the pleasing
struggle to reform the laws, related in a later
chapter. At this period of entire weakness, as
with the rest of Italy, the grandest names were
most in vogue. The captains together took the
name of ' *Il principe*,' and the Council styled
itself ' *Illustre et generale Concilium almæ Reipublicæ illustris libertatis terræ Sancti Marini.*'
Thus, says Sismondi, ' no one addressed his shoe-
maker without calling him " *molto illustre*," and
a petty militia officer was grievously wounded
by being addressed "*Chiarissimo ed eccellentis-
simo*," if he aimed at the title of "*illustrissimo.*"'

The causes of this decadence were many and
various ; in the first place, there was a lack of
regular administration of justice, the Council
did not meet at the stated times, and when they
did, their number was never complete ; secondly,

the lack of public education was a sore deficiency in so small a State, where offices were so frequently changed and there were so few to fill them. Besides this, when anyone found himself educated to a certain standard he went to more extended spheres. And thus it was with the rich, as this barren rock afforded but few enjoyments for those who had put a little money together. Hence absenteeism inflicted all its disadvantages on our State. In addition to this, the number of exiles from other States gave rise to much brigandage around Mount Titanus, and the Government had to go to the expense of keeping up a force, called ' *Salvicondotti*,' to maintain the public safety. Nevertheless, at this time the citizenship of San Marino seems to have been much esteemed, for amongst their number appear the names of many noble families from Rimini, Urbino, and Pesaro.

But before the life-blood of San Marino was entirely extinct a stirring episode was to occur, which combines the authenticity of history with the flavour of romance—an episode which recalled all the latent energies of the State, and to which, perhaps, more than to any other cause, it owes its preservation to this date. And this, perhaps, is of greater interest from the fact that one of the leading characters of Europe in those days was the hero of it. In the next chapter we will investigate this. revival of the constitution, and the circumstances which led to it.

CHAPTER IX.

THE CARDINAL ALBERONI.

'Alberoni,' said Pope Benedict XIV. 'is like a glutton who,
after a good dinner, would fain have some brown bread.'

A VIOLENT attempt made on San Marino's liberty
during the last century, and the means by which
it was perpetrated, must be prefaced by a short
sketch of the life of the perpetrator. When
Europe was pacified by the treaty of Utrecht
in 1713, and the alarm at the power of the
Bourbons was in a measure quelled, Philip V. of
Spain groaned in his weakness at the loss of his
fair Italian possessions. But he did not abandon
all hopes of recovering them, more especially
as those hopes were fostered by the insinuations
of his Prime Minister, who, regardless of all
treaties and rules of honour, again attempted to

break the peace of Europe in order to gain his ends, and this Prime Minister was the Cardinal Egidio Alberoni.

The mushroom growth of this arch-plotter is one of the most curious in history. The illegitimate offspring of a gardener and a spinning-girl at San Lazzaro, near Piacenza, he entered life as apprentice to a cook, and occasionally turned an honest penny by acting in comedies. Finding, however, that the Church offered the most favourable opening for such talents, he became a Sacristan, and then took orders, eventually becoming a Canon and Private Chaplain to the Bishop of Borgo San Donino. Thus, having gained a position from which to start in the political world, his future successes were still more rapid. He had occasion to transact some minor points of detail with the Marshal Vendôme, who was then commanding the French forces in Lombardy in the war of the Spanish succession, about 1703. The Duke recognising Alberoni's transcendent abilities for diplomacy, forthwith chose him as his constant attendant ; and Alberoni received a regular

salary from Louis XIV. of France for his
services, and followed the fortunes of his
new master into the Spanish peninsula, being
frequently brought into connection with the
Court of Spain and the intrigues of Philip V.
By negotiating the marriage between Elizabeth
Farnese, the sister and heiress of the Duke of
Parma, and King Philip, Alberoni put the
crowning point to his fortunes. This act was
most distasteful to the House of Austria and
the rest of Europe, for thereby the Bourbons
got other claims, and fresh opportunities for intrigues on Italian soil. Elizabeth Farnese, however, now found herself all-powerful in Spain;
she ruled her husband and the country through
the assistance of Alberoni, who was nominated
successively a member of the Council of State,
Bishop of Malaga, and Primate of Spain. The
Primate's first step was to restore the shattered
condition of Spain, its army, navy, and finance,
and having in a measure succeeded, he forthwith
threw himself headlong into plots for breaking
the treaty of Utrecht, and re-establishing the
Spanish rule in Italy.

It is curious to follow out the depths of Alberoni's policy against the nations whose interference he feared in his plans. In England he fomented the risings in favour of the Old Pretender, in France he excited the Protestants of the south to rebellion, whilst against Austria he is found to have been in direct correspondence with Ragatschy in Transylvania, and with the Sultan, which obliged the Emperor to re-call Prince Eugène from his command in Italy. Having thus given his enemies plenty of occupation, Alberoni secretly manned a fleet at Barcelona and proceeded to seize Sardinia, which was badly protected, and with a second fleet he came down upon Sicily. But Europe was by this time roused against him; he was everywhere cried down as a robber, a pirate, a breaker of the peace of nations. The despoiled King Victor Amadeo of Savoy hurried to all the Courts of Europe, and by his exertions got up the quadruple alliance against Spain, between England, France, Austria, and the Low Countries.

The hatred against Alberoni was universal;

his own master hated him for his machinations
with his wife; the Pope, Clement XI., hated his
busy Cardinal, whom he had only raised to the
purple on the entreaties of Elizabeth Farnese;
the nations all hated him for his cunning; and,
finally, Elizabeth herself began to hate him for
his domineering manner; and then, in 1719,
the favourite was driven from Spain execrated
by all, and with him went his plans of Spanish
aggrandisement. Alberoni then took to defending himself by the press, laying the whole blame
of his conduct on the King of Spain's Confessor,
Daubanton, and insinuating that the Pope himself was not altogether averse to it. For this
the Cardinal was to have been had up before
the Inquisition, had not Clement XI. died, conveniently for Alberoni, and the world wondered
to see the face of the Cardinal again in Rome,
voting for the election of Innocent XII., and
again in favour at the Vatican. For some time
he continued to live in Rome, turbulent and
intriguing as ever, until Innocent XII. determined to despatch him as legate to the Romagna,
where, amongst the mountains his scope for

injury would be less, though his desire for intrigues was in no way abated.

The year 1739, a year memorable in the annals of San Marino, found Alberoni, the legate of Innocent's successor, Clement XII., established at Ravenna. Still with the same restless mind, and since his wider schemes of re-annexing Sardinia and Sicily to Spain had failed, he was content to occupy himself with projects for handing down his name to posterity as the annexer of our little Republic to the Holy See.

Meanwhile the affairs of San Marino had been growing rapidly worse and worse. The inhabitants appeared to think that the Government would proceed satisfactorily if left to itself, and the number of the Council had again and again been reduced by law. The rejected ones left their country in disgust, and through a meanness of spirit preferred to see the Pontificate ruling in San Marino, since they themselves had neglected to participate in the government, and hence had been deemed unfit members of it. To these Alberoni was always polite, he likened their Captains to Pietro Gradenigo of

Venice, and easily got them to give their consent to the desired annexation, and on this he built his plans.

It is quite clear that plenty of food was given for Alberoni's schemes by the decadence on Mount Titanus, and he was not slow to avail himself of it. Some criminals condemned by the Republic pleaded that they came under the jurisdiction of the Sacred House of Loreto, near Ancona. To enforce this plea they applied to Alberoni, who immediately ordered the San marinesi to deliver them up. Their refusal to do this so greatly enraged the Cardinal that he lost no time in furthering his plans for depriving them of their liberty. Several innocent Sammarinesi, who were about their business at Ravenna, were arrested; goods which were on their way to San Marino were seized in the transport; and all the approaches to the Republic were blocked up by Alberoni's hired bravos; but more formidable than all was a letter written to Rome in which he painted San Marino in the blackest colours. Thus he wrote: 'San Marino is a very Geneva in the heart of

the Papal States, harbouring the enemies of
God and the Saints alike, a hot-bed of tyrants,
and if any hostile prince should seize it he
would make of it a strong standpoint from
which to attack the Pontifical dominions.
Moreover, San Marino is a beam in the Holy
eyes, a nest of dissensions, robbery, and rapine,
which it is necessary to suppress ; and, moreover, it is the sincere wish of the people to be
incorporated in your Holiness's territory.'

Clement XII. was a feeble octogenarian, and
a man of upright tendency, but entirely under
the control of his nephews, the Cardinals Orsini
and Firrao, who probably wished to carve out
of San Marino a small principality for themselves.[1] Hence they distrusted Alberoni, and
wrote back word to him that they would
visit San Marino themselves, and see whether
the inhabitants were thus eager to deliver up
the reins of government. But above all, his
orders were to use prudence! With such instructions, and his plans being thus foiled,
Alberoni determined not to hesitate, but to

---

[1] Botta, *Istoria d'Italia.*

take the law into his own hands; for revenge
he would have, and his custom was not to be
scrupulous in his ways of obtaining it. Out of
the predatory bands and ruffians of Romagna,
Alberoni proceeded to form a little army for
his enterprise of annexing San Marino to the
Pope's dominions, whether the Pope or the
inhabitants wished it or no.

It was a sorry day for the peaceful Republicans when Alberoni appeared at Serravalle
with his followers, and demanded the surrender
of everything, in the name of the Pope. Some
surrendered unconditionally, some fled to the
church, some remained in sullen silence in the
houses, whilst others fled from their native rock,
and sought refuge and assistance from the
sister Republic of Venice.

From Alberoni's own account we gather
that he assembled all who had thus unconditionally surrendered, and took their votes for
the unanimous submission of the whole Republic;
a deed of surrender was drawn up in the Borgo,
and on October 25 Alberoni took possession of
the Castle in the name of the Pope, and from

the tower of the Rocca was seen floating in the pure air of liberty the banner of Papal slavery. On the following day a ceremony of entire submission was planned by the Cardinal; it was to take place before the altar of the

CITADEL OF SAN LEO.

patron Saint, before the very threshold of liberty. A choral service was to be held, with all the pomp of sacerdotal magnificence; the Captains and leading inhabitants were to take the oath of allegiance to the Papal See; whilst outside the temple were posted a number of

Alberoni's soldiers in case of any disturbance. And thus all was arranged according to the Cardinal's heart.

Before the assembled multitude two or three hurriedly took the oath, intimidated by all they saw, the choir chanted magnificently in response, and all seemed to be passing off most smoothly. When, however, it came to the turn of the Captain Giangi, he thus responded bravely to the Cardinal, 'On the first of October I swore fealty to my legitimate Prince, the Republic of San Marino, which oath I confirm, and thus I swear.' These noble sentiments were followed by Guiseppe Onofri, who stated in addition that he was a Sammarinese and not a Roman; whilst one Girolamo Gozi turned complacently towards the Cardinal, and, quoting Scripture, exclaimed, 'May this cup pass from me; I never have disgraced my patron saint, and I never will.' Upon which all took up the cry of '*Viva la libertà!*' until the whole edifice resounded.

Upon this ebullition of feeling the worthy Cardinal entirely lost his self-respect, his face

looked awful, and his language was still more
so, as, says the chronicler of these events, 'it
was an anger more befitting a gardener of
Piacenza than an Ex-Prime Minister of Spain,
a Prince of the Roman Church, and a papal
legate. And so grave was this excess of pas-
sion that the priests were alarmed, and hastily
finished the ceremony amidst a confusion and
hubbub which did not belong to religion, or
to an assembly deliberating on the gravest
affairs of State.'

After this exhibition of truly Spartan
heroism, it is most mortifying to have to relate
that on the following day the Council in deliberation determined to present their humble
submission to Alberoni. It is a fact slurred
over by most of the Republican eulogists, but
still the document is extant to attest to the
craven-heartedness of the Councillors who felt
it their duty to ' protest their vassalage and to
beg for mercy ;' and this document, moreover,
amongst other signatures bears that of a
' Giangi,' not the same, however, who had
spoken out so bravely in the church, for

Alberoni had carefully lodged the non-jurors in prison. Certainly the odds against them were fearful, and their dismay excusable, yet, nevertheless, the story reads much better for San Marino when this abject submission is left out altogether.

In this state of entire surrender San Marino was a prey to the ruthlessness of its conqueror. Alberoni ruled over the inhabitants as sovereign and legislator. He condemned some to prison, and rifled the houses of others, until at length in their great misery the inhabitants secretly sent off an embassy to the Pope, imploring him to remove the obnoxious Cardinal, and to allow affairs to go on in the same channel as they had done before.

A graphic account of the feelings of the people about this time is found in a letter sent by the noble Sammarinese, Girolamo Gozi, to his son, who was studying in the Papal States. After describing his country's misfortunes, and the Cardinal's severity to those who remained firm to their country, he thus concludes : 'Being assured that his Excellency

would receive us, we went to salute him, and
obtained pardon, with the restitution of our
property, of which, however, we all only received
the remnants, and such things as they did not
want. . . . I am glad you are in good health,
my son; the same is the case with us, though
poor. Be cheerful, for San Marino is of a
truth a great man. My inkstand and silver
powder box are gone, and for a candlestick I
use with all cheerfulness a bottle.'

Another faithful citizen of San Marino,
Antonio Belzoppi by name, on Alberoni's
arrival betook himself to Venice, hoping there
to get assistance for his country. His adventures,
as related, are curious, and run as follows:—
Having escaped down one of the most precipi-
tous slopes of the mountain, Belzoppi made the
best of his way to the Serene Republic, and
when there busied himself much in seeking aid
for his oppressed fellow-countrymen. When
Alberoni discovered this he was exceeding
wroth, and hired myrmidons at Venice to do
away with the obnoxious Belzoppi. One night
whilst the Sammarinese was returning home from

a party on foot, three of these bravos fell upon
him and tried to stab him. Belzoppi, however,
managed to reach his gondola, followed by his
enemies, who had theirs also at hand. Then
ensued a chase down the Grand Canal out into
the open lagune, until at length Belzoppi was
overtaken, and a fierce combat took place, in
which Belzoppi worsted his foes, killing the
bravos and their gondolier with his dagger.
No sooner, however, was he freed from this
danger than a fresh one awaited him through
the upsetting of his gondola, and poor Belzoppi,
who was not expert in the art of swimming,
nearly found a watery grave ; when just as he
was giving himself up for lost, he bethought
himself of his patron saint, and called on him
for help. Belzoppi then relates how he saw
the clouds open suddenly, and San Marino's
face appeared looking down upon him as he
struggled on; from that moment he could swim
quite easily, and reached the land without any
further difficulty. This circumstance soon became well known, and all the noblest and
wealthiest Venetians rivalled each other in

showing him civilities. Nay, even they became
so anxious to be related to him that many
offered him their daughters in marriage. But
Antonio Belzoppi, though not blessed with this
world's goods, had a large and faithful heart;
he remembered his wife and children at San
Marino, and returned thither after Alberoni's
tyranny was overpast. an object of almost
veneration to his countrymen, who frequently
raised him to the dignity of Captain and to the
post of prophet amongst them.

Alberoni, before taking his departure from
Mount Titanus, left a governor thereon to carry
out his dictates, and exercise jurisdiction as in
the other Pontifical dominions. But this time
of trial did not last long. The old Pope and
his Cardinal nephews were easily roused to a
sense of Alberoni's enormities by the envoys
from San Marino. Enrico Enriquez, a Nea-
politan, eminent for virtue, and afterwards a
Cardinal, was dispatched by the Pope to investigate the matter, to take the votes of the people,
and if so be they wished it to annul the acts of
Alberoni, but in all things to use his right

judgment. Moreover, he was empowered to rectify the evils which had sprung up in our little State prior to Alberoni's occupation, and to establish the old principles of government under which Mount Titanus had spent so many happy centuries.

It was with unfeigned delight that the Sammarinesi heralded the arrival of Enriquez amongst them. Every inhabitant of Mount Titanus was scrutinised and catechised, monks, nuns, and priests included, in all of whom the love of their native liberty was pre-eminent. No Geneva was here found, as Alberoni suggested, but a community as it exists to-day, a humble-minded, priest-trodden people, with curious ideas about freedom of legislature, which so rarely goes hand-in-hand with religious servitude. But, as Girolamo Gozi said, ' San Marino was indeed a great man,' and experience had taught these shrewd mountaineers that it was safer to owe allegiance to a dead saint than to a living Pope.

In the reports sent by Enriquez to headquarters, the Pope could hardly be compli-

mented to hear that 'there were few lovers of
Roman sovereignty, but many lovers of liberty;'[1]
whilst, at the same time, he stated that this appeared to him not a fierce, but a quiet Republic,
on which liberty had been born and flourished
for many centuries, and was not yet so degenerate as not to be able to throw off those vices
which had taken seed therein; and that·Rome
could not do better than allow San Marino to
live as it had done before, only asking to be
left alone. Thus it followed that this miserable
interregnum continued only for the space of
three and a half months—a time of grief and
suspense for the inhabitants of Mount Titanus,
but a salutary lesson which stood them in good
stead for the future.

On February 5, 1740, Clement XII. restored in full the liberties of the Republic,
almost with his last breath, for he died on the
following day. His successor, Benedict XIV.,
confirmed these; and together these two Popes
are almost worshipped as benefactors of the
State. Certain it is that, during this period,

---

[1] Botta, *Istoria d'Italia.*

San Marino owed much to the clemency of the
Pontiffs; but Alberoni had become a character
of such world-wide notoriety that the Popes
were probably only too glad of so easy a means
of proving to the world their repugnance to his
policy. This, at all events, was a saving point
in the history of San Marino. What Alberoni
sought to effect by a rapid blow would have
been easily brought about by a few more years
of natural decay; and had it been left alone it
is certain that Napoleon, some sixty years later,
would scarcely have been led to say, 'Let us
preserve it as a pattern,' or have done homage
to this little spot like a capricious giant caress-
ing a dwarf.

Great was the delight and enthusiasm displayed on Mount Titanus on receiving the news
of their restored freedom. It was carved in gold
letters on marble, and placed at the entrance
of the city, so that all might read. Pictures
of the Pontiff, and of S. Agatha, on whose day
the propitious event occurred, were painted and
placed on either side of the patron saint in the
Council-room, to assist with their presence the

affairs of State; and February 5 was ordained as a festival for ever, to commemorate the revival of the ancient *régime*.

A procession leaves the Borgo on the morning of this day, of girls in white, dressed as genii, signifying the different virtues. This procession is preceded by two little girls, dressed also in white, carrying the banner of the Republic, on which is symbolised 'liberty;' another carries the sword and balances, to represent justice; also a band of youths are in attendance, carrying lighted candles, to provide which a legacy was left by a member of the noble House of Gozi. Tradition says that this procession owed its origin to the advice of some neighbouring peasantry, who, on the eve of S. Agatha, saw a like procession wending its mystic way up the sides of the mountain.

Thus it followed that, after the lapse of a hundred years, the zealous inhabitants determined to hold a grand festival and gala to commemorate the event. As February 5 is usually inclement on this mountain top, September 3, the day of San Marino, was chosen for the celebration of this *festa*. To do honour to this occasion San Marino put forth all its energies; wonderful things in balloons and fireworks astonished these retired glens. A piece was written for representation in the theatre; a masked ball was given, and great religious festivals took place in the parish church; and for eight successive days the sacred head of St. Marinus was exposed to receive the kisses of the faithful.

On the minds of the older inhabitants this festival is still deeply impressed as the one great gala day of their lives. When once the tongues of the housewives are loosened on this topic, it behoves the visitor patiently to listen to a description of all the dresses at the masked ball, and how the gaudy tinsel of the genii was unfortunately spoilt by a shower of rain. All this happened nearly forty years ago, but it is still the favourite topic of the aged.

But what of Alberoni during this time? Benedict XIV., no lover of this proud Cardinal, removed him from this district of Romagna to Bologna, where in retirement, and under the

biting influence of lost glory, he published a
work on his conquest of Mount Titanus, in
which he visits the Papacy, the Sacred College,
and our little Republic with all the contumely
which a revengeful spirit could invent. This
led to a literary war, which filled the Vatican
with letters without end, on the subject of San
Marino, and at least had the effect of giving a
notoriety to Mount Titanus, which, prior to this,
had fallen into oblivion ; whilst the constitution recovered from this shock its former position, private disputes were put aside, and the
Republic took out, so to speak, a new lease of
existence.

CHAPTER X.

NAPOLEON IN ITALY.

Quand se lassera-t-on d'inquiéter ces paisibles habitans d'une contrée, qu'on a appelée, un atome politique, et qu'il faut respecter tout atome qu'il est, car là il y a plus de sagesse, de vertu véritable, de prudence et de bon sens que dans tant de contrées qui vantent présomptueusement leurs mérites.—*Artaud de Montor.*

FOR the space of forty years after the peace of Aix-la-Chapelle, in 1748, Italy enjoyed a period of rest, at least from war, though suffering much from the tyranny of her many rulers. The growth of the House of Savoy formed the most marked point of this period. That rule was despotic, but a healthy tone pervaded it ; whilst in Naples the countenance given by the Bourbon sovereigns to all kinds of lawlessness led to a state of anarchy, which made the southern provinces a prey to the greatest misery.

An undercurrent of liberal principles, how-

ever, as in France, led to the foundation of
every species of secret societies. But that which
led to the French Revolution never fully developed itself on Italian soil. The Carbonari and
Freemasons were kept down with a strong hand
by the Popes and other despots, and the want
of unity in this case proved a safeguard for
Italy against the bitterness of the Revolution,
which nearly ruined France. Curious papers
have lately come to light, which prove that the
Freemasons intended to seize San Marino, and
form it into a basis of operations. The Cardinal Chiaramonti, afterwards Pius VII., and then
in close connection with the Court of Pius VI.,
discovered this plot in 1790, and saved the
Republic. He wrote from Imola, stating that
the Freemasons had taken minute information
as to the situation and fortifications of Mount
Titanus, with a view to seizing it. Poor Sam-
maranesi! Quite ignorant of the wiles of their
enemies around them, they went on in innocent enjoyment of their self-government. Their
annals never show any feelings of alarm about
this time ; and had it not been for a kindly

supervision from without, the tragedy of Alberoni might have been re-enacted with twofold
misery.

But other and more stirring events were
shortly to awaken Italy from its state of depres-
sion, its miserable plots and counterplots. An
echo of freedom was heard from across the
Alps, that degenerate and transient freedom
which shook France to its basis, but which in
the end laid the foundation of modern society.
In 1796 the northern invaders entered Italy
under General Napoleon Buonaparte, flaunting
the flag of liberty, and inculcating the spirit of
revolution, as they had done in France, when
rulers and despots were overthrown, and priests
and prayer-books were scattered to the winds.

The glorious victories of the French general
were reported to the inhabitants of Mount
Titanus, and they trembled in their insignificance to hear of Lodi, of the fall of Venice, and
other marvellous exploits, and they were so far
imbued with the spirit of the times as to give
up their noble families.[1] But otherwise they

[1] *Vide* chapter xiv.

could only wait to be swallowed up in Napoleon's chaotic abyss.

When, on February 7, 1797, the invincible general was lodged at Pesaro, and on his being jeeringly asked what should be done with the Republic of San Marino, he exclaimed, '*Con-*

SAN MARINO FROM ACQUAVIVA.

servons-la comme un échantillon de république,' and with this the existence of San Marino was preserved.   For Napoleon was not then the Napoleon of Brumaire 18, or of 1804 ; he still had some pretensions at form, and to seize San Marino would have been an anachronism, and a folly for a man in his position, and with the views he then professed.

To certify his brotherly and friendly feeling for the little Republic, Napoleon dispatched his friend and companion, Monge, a truly curious man, who had left the post of professor of mathematics and physics, and inventor of cannons, to join in the construction of Napoleon's fortunes. He followed Buonaparte in his campaigns in Italy and Egypt, and occupied many posts of honour in both. But he is chiefly celebrated for his keen eye for the value of antiquities. To him, rather than to Napoleon, is due the credit of devastating so many of the Italian museums, and carrying off the works of art he there found to beautify the galleries of Paris. Monge also published many valuable works on various scientific subjects, and, judging from his harangue to the Republicans of San Marino, his flow of language must have been great. As Monge's interview with the Council of San Marino forms a curious specimen of forensic blarney on the one hand, and uncultured astuteness on the other, I will here

transcribe it, as it is entered in the archives, word
for word. Introduced before the Council of
Sixty, bearing Napoleon's message of peace, he
thus thought fit to address our hardy mountaineers. 'That liberty which, in the palmy days
of Athens and Sparta, transformed Greece into
a people of heroes; that liberty, which, in the
times of the Republic, wrought prodigies at
Rome, which, during the short interval of its
existence in some of the Italian towns, renewed the sciences and the arts, and illuminated
Florence; that liberty, I say, was almost
entirely banished from Europe; it alone
existed at San Marino, where, through your
wisdom, citizens, and more especially through
your virtues, its asylum has been defended
through so long a course of years. The French
nation, after being enlightened for a century,
began to blush at its slavery, and is now free;
all Europe, blinded to its own interests, and
above all, to the interests of mankind at large,
coalesced and armed itself against her. Her
neighbours covenanted together for a partition
of her territory; all her frontiers were simul-

taneously attacked, her fortresses and her ports
were in the power of the enemy, and that
which afflicted her most was the fact that in
France herself a precious part of her population
spread civil war, and forced her to strike blows
which fell on her own head. Alone in the
midst of so great a storm, without experience,
arms, or leaders, France rushed to her frontiers,
and offered resistance on every side, and on
every side was triumphant; then the wisest of
her enemies retreated, and the success of her
army obliged the rest to implore for peace,
which they obtained. Now, indeed, there remain but three, and they are infatuated, and
listen to no counsel, but that of pride, of
jealousy, and of hatred. One of the French
armies has now entered Italy, and has overthrown four Austrian armies, one after the
other, carrying liberty into this fair land, and
covering itself with immortal honour, almost
under your very eyes. The French Republic,
with regret at so much bloodshed, and content
at having given a grand example to the universe,
now proposes a peace, which it could dictate.

Would you credit it, my citizens? everywhere these propositions are rejected with scorn, or eluded with craft. The Italian army, to gain that peace, is obliged to pursue its enemies, and to pass close by your territories. I am deputed by General Buonaparte, in the name of the French Republic, to assure the Republic of San Marino of his peaceful intentions, and of his inviolable friendship. Citizens, the political constitution of the people who surround you is open to change ; and if any part of your frontier is absolutely necessary to you, I am charged by the General-in-Chief to beg of you to let him know. It will be with the greatest readiness that he will thereby enable the French Republic to give you a clear proof of its sincere friendship ; as for myself, I am content to have been the organ in a mission, which must be so pleasing to two Republics, and which affords me an occasion to prove to you the veneration with which you inspire all true lovers of liberty.'

From Napoleon's subsequent conduct we can but argue that he wished to make San Marino

the centre of one of those numerous Republics
with which he stocked Italy, and out of which
he looked to carving kingdoms and principalities for his relations and deserving generals.
Thus, shortly after, we find this part of Italy
rejoicing in the name of the Cisalpine Republic,
whilst there were also set up the Ligurian, the
Cispadane, and the Tiberine Republics, with
Genoa, Bologna, and Rome as their respective
capitals. Naples followed in the next year as
the Parthenopæan Republic. And some few
years after this we find Joseph Buonaparte,
and after him Joachim Murat as successive
kings of this last, whilst Eugène Beauharnais
ruled over the Cisalpine and Ligurian Republics
combined. Whatever may have been his intentions with regard to San Marino, certain it
is that all danger was warded off by the shrewd
and politic answer of Antonio Onofri, who was
then the leading spirit on Mount Titanus. An-
swering Monge's speech in flowing strain,
Onofri thus prefaced his refusal of this brilliant
offer. ' Your army, and its young and valiant
leader, who unites the talents of genius with the

virtues of the hero, follow in the steps of Hannibal, and recall the wonders of ancient days ; your eyes are now turned on a spot of ground where the *débris* of primitive liberty has sought an asylum, and on which the precision of Sparta is more conspicuous than the elegance of Athens.' But, as of yore, he continued, San Marino only asked to be left alone, and Monge returned to his master's camp to communicate the humble but sagacious reply of the Sammarinesi.

Thus another great danger to San Marino's existence was averted. Had they been tempted by Napoleon's specious offer, our Republicans would without doubt have been swamped in the future arrangement of kingdoms, whereas by retaining their pristine insignificance, they were able to treat with the other Republics and kingdoms as they came into existence in the position they had always held for so many centuries.

Shortly after Monge's visit, Napoleon vouchsafed to write himself to the Republic a letter, dated from Modena, February 28, 1797, in

which he says: 'The citizen Monge has described to me, citizens, the touching picture
which your little Republic presented to him.
I have given orders that the citizens of San
Marino shall be exempt from all contributions,
and respected throughout the French Republic.
I have also given orders to the General
Salmquet, whose head-quarters are at Rimini, to
send you four field-pieces, of which I make you
a present in the name of the French Republic.
He will also place at your disposition a thousand measures of corn, which will stock your
Republic until the harvest time. I pray you to
believe, citizens, that in all circumstances I
shall use all my endeavours to prove to the
inhabitants of San Marino the esteem and
consideration with which I sign myself—
BUONAPARTE.'

In reply to this gracious epistle, Onofri said
that they would gladly receive the cannons and
corn, but only on payment for the same.[1] The
Sammarinesi begged for some extension of
commercial interests; and on this point alone

---

[1] Botta, *Istoria d'Italia.*

did they solicit the assistance of the invincible general. It is characteristic of Napoleon and his promises, that, as a sequel to this episode, it must be added, that the cannons and corn never found their way to Mount Titanus, and no further mention at the time was made of our little Republic, a circumstance which it by no means regretted.

It was well for the inhabitants of Mount Titanus that at this time they had so prudent and trustworthy a citizen and adviser as Antonio Onofri, a descendant of the citizen who spoke up so boldly before Alberoni. Onofri was endowed with all the requisites of a great statesman, though his sphere was small. During all the troublous years at the commencement of this century Onofri steered his little bark through the various tempests with admirable tact and precision. Whether at Rome, Paris, or Vienna he made himself respected, and by his presence protected his little country from being engulfed in any of those sweeping treaties which followed the fall of Napoleon's fortunes. In 1802 we find him

conducting an embassy to Milan, and forming
for San Marino a highly advantageous commercial treaty with the Cisalpine Republic,
whilst later on in the same year, Napoleon as
first Consul President of the Italian Republic
orders this little embassy to form part of
the Corps Diplomatique; on December 5 the
body of simple mountaineers were presented at
the Tuileries with the ministers of all foreign
Powers; on the 12th they were honoured
with a formal audience at St. Cloud; and were
received by Napoleon with every mark of
pleasure and kindness.

When Napoleon was formally crowned King
of Italy at Milan, the inhabitants of San Marino
felt alarmed, lest the mantle of clemency which
was displayed by the general and consul should
not continue to adorn the sovereign. But
Onofri was again received with cordiality, and
the old promises of protection were again renewed. Not only was Napoleon friendly
towards San Marino, but the same spirit seemed
to actuate those under him. When in 1808,
Eugène, as Viceroy of Italy, found himself near

the heights of Mount Titanus, he wrote to the Captains with his own pen in answer to their embassy of respect. And Joachim Murat, too, from his throne at Naples, treated with every mark of kindness the embassy sent by San Marino to congratulate him on his accession.

After the Congress of Vienna had settled Europe to a certain degree, and the various countries began to rearrange themselves after their vast upheaval, Pius VII., the old Cardinal Chiaramonti, who had watched over San Marino's interests when threatened by the freemasons, entered into the old amicable relations of protector and guardian of our little State, as the Popes had been of yore. Thus, after this general pacification, in taking a glance at the position of Italy, we find San Marino the only Republic now in existence. Venice had gone, and Genoa was now in the possession of the House of Savoy, whilst throughout the length and breadth of the land there existed only two native sovereigns, namely the Pope and the King of Sardinia. 'Young Italy,' as represented by Giuseppe Mazzini and his Republican outburst, and constitutional Italy as represented by Charles Albert, were as yet only looming in the distance.

A few years of unbroken peace, if not of contentment, served to soothe men's heated brains, and but few foreign complications disturbed San Marino's serenity until 1824, when Leo XII. was seated on the chair of St. Peter. Leo XII. was a pompous, disagreeable man; a Pope who wished to see the stately days of the Middle Ages restored to the Papacy. He hated the advance of science and art, he hated all movers in the way of freedom, and as for Republicanism, it was in his eyes a most heinous sin. By the assistance of the Jesuits, and his Legate, Rivarola, Leo managed to keep up a regular system of espionage, which put a check on the Carbonari for a time, but fanned the secret flames which were to have their outburst in the days of his successor, Pius IX.

A means of re-embroiling Europe in war was constantly looked for by the plenipotentiaries at the Vatican, and our small Republic inadvertently was near providing them with

their object. A small faction on Mount Titanus
was anxious for annexation to the Papal States,
but by far the most numerous party, headed
by Onofri, preferred the ancient *régime*, and on
the occasion of Leo XII.'s accession sent a
congratulatory embassy, whilst the other faction filled the waste-paper baskets of the
Vatican with earnest entreaties for annexation.
The Holy Father flatly refused to receive the
deputation which was sent, alleging as his excuse that he would have received an embassy
composed entirely of the subjects of San Marino,
but as the message had been entrusted to some
residents in Rome, he felt obliged to refuse to
receive a deputation of his own subjects.[1]
Others maintain that the Pontiff was so bothered
by the constant letters he had received that he
refused to admit the deputation in a fit of
anger. Be this as it may, it was soon noised
abroad ; Russia, Prussia, and England were informed that the Holy See was anxious to break
existing treaties. Men vaguely reported that
the Cardinal della Sommaglia, Leo's adviser,

[1] Artaud de Montor, *Life of Leo XII.*

and a godson of Alberoni, was anxious to perform what his godfather had been unable to
effect. But taking into consideration that Cardinal della Sommaglia was eighty years of age,
and that Alberoni had merely chanced to hold
him at the font, little ambition of this kind can
have existed in the Cardinal's head.

Again, in this difficulty Antonio Onofri
stepped forward. Being a citizen of San Marino
the Pope was willing to receive him as a deputy ;
and the Russian Minister, M. Le Chevalier
Italinski, the French Chargé-d'Affaires, and
Prince Doria, at once set to work to patch up
the mischief created. For so tender were the
threads which held together the peace of
Europe at this time, that even the occupation
of so insignificant a spot as San Marino would
have broken them.

The grateful little Republic presented these
three pacificators with the '*patriciate*,'[1] and the
French King authorised his Chargé d'Affaires to
accept it, and at the same time to tender his
sincere feelings of respect to a Republic which

[1] *Vide* chapter xiv.

had 'survived its more powerful sisters, by its prudence and disinterestedness, since the year 520.'[1]

It is a good instance of Onofri's tact and good judgment, that, when it was in his power to expose the names of his fellow-countrymen who had wished for annexation to Rome, he concealed them, thereby avoiding further disturbances. He burnt all the papers which implicated them, and was content solely to keep his eye upon them until his death, which occurred shortly afterwards. He died deeply lamented by his countrymen, who erected a fine marble monument to his memory in their parish church, and thereon inscribed him as 'father of his country.' With him, too, died his honoured name, and one of the most noble and well-beloved families of San Marino became thereby extinct.

[1] Artaud de Montor.

CHAPTER XI.

THE NINETEENTH CENTURY.

If Italy, instead of being a Pantheon of memories and great works, were a little less rich in art, but more robust, and if she had strong and industrious citizens, she certainly would cease to be the slave of the foreigner, stronger and more industrious than herself.—GARIBALDI.

THE story of San Marino for the last fifty years is one of extraordinary peace and content-ment; whilst the rest of Italy was convulsed by her struggle for liberty, San Marino looked on complacently, occasionally catching some breeze from the surrounding tempest; but, by adhering to a policy of strict neutrality, and never mixing in the affairs of others, our Republic succeeded in maintaining its independence.

On one occasion, when there was some talk of joining San Marino to another State, the chivalrous but unfortunate Charles X. of France

remarked to M. de Vitelle, 'all States ought to
help each other mutually, the strong ought to
support the weak, and if such an event should
happen, I should declare myself the defender of
San Marino, and should plant the French standard on its towers, and it would be the worse
for whoever might approach it.'[1]

Meanwhile the power of autocracy was
brought to a crisis in Italy by the intense
bigotry of Pope Gregory XVI.; he opposed by
all the means in his power the advance of
science and art, and looked upon railways and
telegraphs as machinations of the devil; he
was entirely under the control of his Jesuitical
advisers, and being without men or money to
carry out his plans, was obliged to throw himself wholly into the hands of Austria.

The idea of freeing Italy from the foreign
yoke gave birth to the genius of Mazzini and
his followers, who, carried away by enthusiasm,
soon shot beyond the wishes of Charles Albert
and the moderate party, and consequently this
burst of liberal feeling was doomed to an early

[1] de Barghou-Fortrion.

death, and Mazzini found himself banished from
his country. However, with the example of
Europe before her, and the encouragement of a
liberal Pope in Pius IX., Italy could not help
being led on to throw off the yoke of her many
tyrants, and in 1848 there was a general eager-
ness displayed throughout the land to drive the
foreigner from the country. Pius himself blessed
the banners of revolt, and sent the Papal forces
to join the popular cause. Daniele Manin led
on the Venetians to deeds of valour, whilst
Garibaldi with his irregular bands kept up a
species of guerilla warfare in the north. But
the Austrian power was still too strong, and the
defeat of Custoza, followed by the defection of
the Pope from the side of freedom, entirely
ruined the hopes of the moderate party. Nevertheless the Republicans still took heart. Pius IX.
was obliged to flee to Gaeta from Rome on the
box of a carriage, dressed as a common priest,
and the Romans sent for Garibaldi to undertake
the defence of their city and their infant Republic. For four weeks the Roman Republicans
and Garibaldi's volunteers held out against the

French attack; but at length, after a desperate attempt, on the night of June 30, 1849, the Eternal City was compelled to seek a truce, and the French entered on July 2. Meanwhile Garibaldi and Mazzini made their escape, and the former, with his motley crew of followers, hurried northwards towards Venice to the assistance of Manin, who still kept up the spirit of revolt in the lagunes.

At the head of this band of bravos, Garibaldi hoped, by opening a passage towards Tuscany, to revive the dying flame of liberty still existing in the heart of the Apennines. After unheard of perils, he reached Macerata, and from thence passed on to St. Angelo in Vado, where, under the very eyes of Mount Titanus, he suffered his final defeat at the hands of the Austrians.

With such a harbour of refuge at hand, Garibaldi lost no time in despatching his quarter-master before him to San Marino to announce his arrival, and to request a safe passage and victuals for his troops. The Captains and Council, after much deliberation, felt obliged to refuse, though they would

willingly have done all in their power for this
kindred spark of liberty, so nearly extinguished.
However, they felt that with the Austrians in
their rear the troops of Garibaldi would have
brought ruin on their little State, and hence
they were obliged to send a reluctant refusal,
at the same time promising to place food for
them outside the Republican precincts.

Garibaldi, however, defeated as he was on
all sides, had no other course to pursue, and
hardly had they worded their response before
the trembling citizens found the General and his
followers with them in the Borgo. A curious
spectacle, indeed, did they present, but pic-
turesque amid their squalor and dejection, with
their red shirts all in rags, 1,500 infantry and
300 cavalry in all. Dejected and terrified by
their late misfortunes, no military discipline
now reigned in this motley group of old men and
boys ; some sank to the ground with exhaustion.
whilst others stood by smiling with unnatural
composure. There were many women, also,
amongst them, who had clung to their hus-
bands, sons, and brothers, through all their

scenes of misery, death, and danger. Their beauty was faded through excess of hunger and exposure; but from their weary eyes streamed the hazy brightness of inspiration. Such were the women who swelled the ranks of the Parisian commune,—a morbid careworn crew, who filled with pity the hearts of our Republicans. The advent of this band was a great episode in the uneventful lives of the Sammarinesi, and one on which they still love to dwell.

Garibaldi himself, and one or two of his followers, went straight up to the Città, and to the government house, where he offered to deliver up his arms, and implored victuals and a lodging for his band. 'All hail to the fugitives!' said the Captain Belzoppi, 'in such a position we will receive you,' and he forthwith gave orders that food should be distributed amongst the men in the Borgo, and that Garibaldi himself with his wife, who accompanied him, should be lodged with all hospitality in the Franciscan convent near the gate, after having extorted from the General a promise that if the Germans did not attack him during this respite he would not attack them. After partaking of the hospitality offered him, Garibaldi then went down to the Borgo to address his men, exhorting them to forbear from all acts of violence, as they were on friendly ground, and at the same time posted up the following order on the peristyle of the parish church :

'Soldiers,—We have arrived in a land of refuge ; we must maintain an irreproachable conduct towards our generous hosts, since it will gain for us the respect merited by our misfortunes. From the present moment I release all my companions in arms from every engagement, leaving them free to re-enter private life. But I would remind them that it is better to die than to live as slaves to a foreigner.

'GARIBALDI.'

Meanwhile, the Austrians from the side of Rimini threatened San Marino, as conniving at Garibaldi's escape. So with great haste the Republic despatched the Secretary of State to intercede for a capitulation in favour of Garibaldi, and for their own safety. In his hurried departure this official had neglected to adorn himself in a manner befitting his office, and was arrested as a spy by an Austrian soldier; however, on being taken before the Archduke Ernest, who was in command of the army, and on his credentials being examined, the unfortunate Secretary of State was released from his quandary, and treated with all due respect.

On the subject of Garibaldi's band, however, the Archduke was obdurate; he promised to spare in every way the Republic, and apologised for inadvertently having crossed the frontier, but at the same time he felt obliged to demand the surrender of Garibaldi and his followers.

After some length of time, and more than one message passing between the Sammarinesi and the Austrians, who refused to enter into direct negotiations with Garibaldi, the Archduke Ernest agreed to give conditions of the severest nature, obliging Garibaldi at once to depart to America. The General, however, whilst his soldiers slept, and whilst the Republicans were unconsciously dreaming of the difficulties of to-morrow, determined to effect his

escape, with his wife, and 150 of his most
trusted followers. He thus quietly stole away
from our Republic's territories by way of the
marshes of the Comachio towards Venice,
leaving the following laconic note on his bed-
room table: 'The conditions imposed on me
by the Austrians are unacceptable, and therefore we cease to encumber your territory.—
GARIBALDI.'

At the break of day the remnant of Garibaldi's band awoke to find themselves deserted,
and great was their dismay, and loud were
their threats against those who had deceived
them. Refreshed by their night's rest, they felt
prepared to receive the Austrian attack, and consulted as to whether it would not be advisable
to occupy Mount Titanus; at all events, each man
affirmed that he preferred death to surrender.
The Sammarinesi, in this dire emergency, at once
closed their gates, and sent messages for assistance to the Austrians, whilst the Garibaldians
cooled their angered brains by counsel, and
Colonel Jacchi, their leader, prevailed upon
them not to requite their benefactors with

bloodshed. Thus, somewhat appeased, and becoming convinced that life was more sweet than a foolhardy death, the band at length determined to accept the Republic's protection, and to deliver up their arms in peace to the Sam-

THE PORTA FRANCISCANA.

marinesi, which ceremony took place at the Porta Franciscana with all the customary formalities, and the open-hearted Republicans presented each man with two paoli,[1] and a passport for Rimini; and thus, after exchanges of compli-

[1] Paolo = 5d.

ments between the two classes of Republicans, San Marino was released from its unpleasant visitors.

The Austrians, however, were much exasperated when they found that Garibaldi had finally escaped out of their clutches; and by way of revenge they seized the Garibaldians on their way to Rimini, and their paoli and their passports to boot; and it required much pacification and persuasion on the part of the Captain whom the Sammarinesi hurriedly despatched, before the Archduke would acquit our Republicans of having connived at the escape of Austria's arch-enemy. At length, however, the Austrian general was appeased, and nothing but polite messages passed between the Austrians and the Sammarinesi; the Archduke asking leave to remove his soldiers into more comfortable quarters, and the Sammarinesi inviting him to bring them all to the Borgo, whilst the Archduke himself was to be lodged in the house of the Conte Borghese in the Città. Nothing loath to accept this hospitality, the Austrian general took this opportunity to rest his army for a few days, and made himself most agreeable to the inhabitants, receiving deputations, and enquiring into the constitutions of the Republic, gracefully vouchsafing to admire everything he saw therein. Much, however, as they may personally have liked their guest, the Sammarinesi thought fit to offer up a Te Deum in their church on his departure, as a thanksgiving for their escape from so many dangers. For some time, however, the rear of Garibaldi's followers, who had managed to escape from the Austrians, lurked about in the neighbouring mountains. This was the cause of some petty acts of brigandage, and a good deal of annoyance to the Republic, but it was eventually put down, and all went on again most smoothly.

But this little episode in their history cost the Republic no small sum of money; their commissariat was drained again and again, and the inhabitants not unfrequently felt the pangs of hunger, having so many mouths to fill, as, of course, there was no one to repay them for their outlay; but they were contented in their humble

minds to have been instrumental in saving the
life of one so dear to Italian freedom as Garibaldi.

Another breeze with the Austrian invaders
ruffled the serenity of San Marino, when, after
the entire rout of the Republican party in Rome,
forty of them came to Mount Titanus, as a harbour of refuge. However, the Prolegate Bedini,
of Bologna, sent at once to demand the restitution of these men in the name of Austria; and
poor San Marino, recognising its own helpless-
ness, but feeling grieved at the act of injustice
thus imposed upon them, returned an answer to
the Prolegate that he might come and fetch the
men himself, for it would never arrest them
on its own account; and as for two of the
forty, who happened to be Sammarinesi, they
flatly refused to deliver them up.

Pope Pius IX., with all his liberal protesta-
tions at the outset of his pontificate, soon
checked his liberal career by throwing himself
into the arms of Austria, and finally receiving
aid from Napoleon III. He likewise, after
these backslidings, evinced a great enmity

towards our Republic, eagerly looking for an opportunity to appropriate it as his own. Pius IX. had, of a truth, sorely suffered from republicanism, and we can hardly wonder that he abhorred the name, and considered San Marino an evil precedent in the very heart of his dominions; consequently Pius was nothing loath to seize an opportunity afforded him by the assassination of one Gian Battista Bonelli, an honourable and respected Sammarinese. The reason for this crime, and the perpetrator thereof, continued to be unknown to the world, and hence gave rise to every species of groundless suspicion; thereby Pius obtained an excellent excuse for appropriating our Republic on the score of misgovernment. To carry out his plans, the Pope asked the assistance of Tuscany; but again a Buonaparte saved San Marino. Napoleon III flatly refused to allow this occupation, and ordered his ambassador at Rome, M. de Reyneval, to send someone to inquire closely into the state of affairs on Mount Titanus. This office was entrusted to the care of M. Baudet, and on his examination and his

report to Napoleon proving satisfactory, the
Emperor encouraged our Republic by address-
ing their embassy to Paris as follows: 'Keep
your innocent customs, my citizens, and continue in the path which you have trodden for
so many centuries, and always count on my
protection.' To the gracious assistance of the
Buonaparte dynasty San Marino owed a second
time its safety and the continuation of its
ancient freedom.

About this time a learned man, the Count
Borghese, took up his residence in almost
the highest house on Mount Titanus, where
he could pursue his studies unmolested. He
lived, as his biographer states, like a bee, who
descended into the busy scenes of life to
collect materials for his honey—a honey, alas!
of no sweet flavour for the world at large, but
presenting the very aroma of Parnassus to the
antiquary. Borghese made a vast collection of
Greek and Roman coins, which now forms the
nucleus of the great numismatic collection in
the museum at Naples; and he wrote in his
seclusion numerous pamphlets and classifications

of the same, piles of which lie in hopeless dis-
order in the Sammarinese Museum. Besides
this the Count collected epitaphs, and was well
skilled in deciphering inscriptions upon stones.
He died in 1860, in his house on Mount Titanus,
and his memory is held in great esteem, as that
of a good citizen should be amongst the Republicans, though his literary attainments are
not treated with the respect they merited, being
at the same time beyond the comprehension
and beneath the notice of our hardy mountaineers.

On the accession of the House of Savoy to
the entire rule of Italy, Luigi Cibrario, a minor
satellite, whose special brilliancy was somewhat
eclipsed and held in check by Cavour, Mas-
simo d'Azeglio, and others, took San Marino
under his particular protection, being as he
was a citizen of the Republic, and at the
same time occupying many important posts in
the Government of Victor Emmanuel. Thus
Cibrario obtained for San Marino terms which
the Republicans would have found it hard to
procure without his assistance. In chapter xiii.

I shall state at greater length the advantages
which thereby accrued to our little State.
The Republicans were by no means unthankful
to Cibrario for his trouble, and heaped upon
him all the small honours within their reach.
Besides being made a member of their Equestrian order,[1] Cibrario was, as a mark of special
favour, allowed to quarter the three towers of
the Republic in his own coat of arms; and a
slab commemorating his achievements on San
Marino's behalf is inserted in the walls of the
Council Chamber.

On the occasion of the opening of the railway from Bologna to Ancona, our Republic's
repose was doubtless a little disturbed by thus
being brought within twelve miles of an inven-
tion which could carry them to the uttermost
parts of the earth. The track of steam, as the
train is hurried on its way along the coast of
the Adriatic, is descried for miles from San
Marino's eagle nest, forming a curious contrast for the imagination to dwell upon, whilst
carried back by all around to ages long gone

[1] *Vide* chapter xiv.

by. A deputation was sent to congratulate Victor Emmanuel at the opening ceremony, and at the grand dinner given afterwards the King caused the humble Sammarinesi to be seated on his right.

Although from external appearances the inhabitants of Mount Titanus do not seem to have taken much advantage of the facilities for locomotion placed within their reach, and though but few modern inventions, and but a limited number of the world's busy sight-seers have reached its summit, nevertheless the iron way has been the means of allowing the Sammarinesi to take a share in the great fever for Exhibitions of this nineteenth century. San Marino was to be found in the great 'Street of Nations,' under the same roof with her sister of Andorra and the principality of Monaco, at Paris in 1878. Though her productions were humble, some of them at least had the merit of originality. All the books and pamphlets that ever had been written on the Republic were collected together, and so placed that those 'who ran might read.' Specimens of agriculture likewise adorned this room, whilst on the walls appeared their stamps and coins. But, above all, a coat of arms, wrought by a native workman out of native stone, was an object of their special pride.

But though they could do but little to vie with the wealth of Europe in her gaudy show, yet the very existence of the name of San Marino amongst the rest formed unconsciously one of the greatest curiosities in this hive of nations, and by its appearance there it proved to the world at large that it was no fossil, like most of its less fortunate sisters, but a still living community, in which the elements of an honest and thriving population are still extant.

CHAPTER XII.

HISTORICAL COMPARISONS AND AN UNHISTORICAL TRAGEDY.

Nothing indeed can be a greater instance of the natural love that mankind has for liberty, and of their aversion to arbitrary government, than such a savage mountain covered with people, and the Campagna of Rome almost destitute of inhabitants.— ADDISON, *Travels in Italy.*

HAVING thus traversed the centuries during which this petty State has existed, let us consider the extent of this liberty, and how far San Marino owed subservience to its neighbouring protectors.

In looking around to find a parallel amongst other independent States, we find it hard to hit on any that will compare with San Marino. The Republics of Switzerland have had to fight for the freedom which they possess, and at one time overthrew Charles of Burgundy, the most powerful prince of the period. The old Greek

Republics, though perhaps no larger in extent than Mount Titanus, owned no immediate protectors, but were pitted one against another in continual strife.

Again, various authors draw a comparison between the position of San Marino and that of the commercial towns of Germany, inasmuch as they governed themselves by their own laws, yet at the same time owed fealty to the Empire. But here we have no Swabian or Hanseatic League for mutual protection, and no rich merchants and bankers who could make the Holy Roman Empire tremble.

At the Paris Exhibition, as we have seen, San Marino was represented side by side with its sister Republic of Andorra, which clings to the name of liberty in the valley of Balira, in Catalonia, at the foot of the Pyrenees. This State consists of six parishes, and of about 12,000 inhabitants, united under one Government. It is somewhat junior in origin to that of San Marino, boasting of having received its charter of liberty from Charlemagne, and to have had it renewed again by Louis le

Débonnaire. But here we find the two '*Viguiers,*' or Presidents of the Republic, one elected by France, and the other by the Spanish Bishop of Urgell, under whose protection the Republic is placed. But the French nominee is held of small account, and the virtual authority is executed by the deputy of Spain. This Republic has no code of laws, but the judges follow that used in Catalonia, modified by local customs. Here Napoleon, as at San Marino, condescended to parade his clemency. ' I recall,' said he, ' a miniature Republic, lost in a corner of the Pyrenees, which I respected as a political curiosity.'

In short San Marino is a solecism in the polity of Europe. The offspring of centuries long gone by, it has grown old in its infancy, and from its anomalous position has called forth much criticism from amongst its adversaries and supporters, who treating it in the light of the more modern system of statecraft have missed the very point of its existence.

Its career from first to last is marked out into three distinct phases. *Firstly*, when, in the

troubled centuries before the contest of Guelph
and Ghibelline, the Italians gathered round
any sacred spot, and formed themselves into
communities asserting some mystic and saintly
origin, as a means to escape the encroaching
tyranny of the nobles; during all which time
San Marino had no neighbour strong enough,
and there was no one perhaps who cared, to
appropriate this barren spot. During this
period the social and political condition of
Italy contributed much to the formation of
free communities. The Saracenic and other
invaders encouraged the maintenance of local
militia, and the habit of living in walled cities,
and, receiving no assistance or interference from
the imperial and nominal feudal head, they were
left free to choose what government seemed
best for them. In the twelfth century we find
in Italy about two hundred free communities
or republics, most of which gradually became
absorbed, or subservient to the nobles, who,
on one pretext or another, managed to get
the inhabitants into their power. But from
their peculiar position these communities never

enjoyed entire political independence, they received their franchise, or were under the protection of neighbouring dukes and counts, more or less dominant as circumstances occurred, whilst these dukes and counts were again the feudatories of some distant power, and ranged themselves on the side of Emperor or Pope as they found most suitable for their interests. Hence these early Italian Republics were rather what in modern times would be termed free municipalities, which had received exceptionally liberal charters from their lords paramount. This is the exact character and nature of the government of San Marino, which has been maintained through so many centuries.

This brings us to the *second* phase in the history of our Republic. When Frederic Barbarossa introduced the foreign element into Italy, San Marino found itself under the immediate protection of one of the most warlike and powerful Ghibelline princes, the Counts of Montefeltro, and later the Dukes of Urbino. During this phase in its history its freedom was due most especially to the fact that it was a bulwark between the hostile houses of Montefeltro and Malatesta, and by complete subserviency to the more powerful of these princes it retained its freedom and position until the Montefeltrian Dukes were firmly seated in Romagna. It formed one of the main characteristics of this house that they never encroached on the liberty of their subjects. No more liberal or high-minded race of princes ever governed in Italy, and the existence of San Marino in their very midst is an ample testimony to the policy they pursued.

On the extinction of the line of the Dukes of Urbino,[1] their territories were fused in those of the Holy See, and with this San Marino entered on the *third* phase of its career. By this time it had procured for itself a position which the Popes of those days were unable to break. If Cæsar Borgia had established his rule in Romagna before his father's death, or if Leo X. had succeeded in adding to his family's possessions the Duchy of Urbino, the days of our Republic would have been num-

[1] A.D. 1631.

bered with those of its protectors, for, with
the rest of Romagna, Cæsar Borgia possessed
Mount Titanus; but fortunately for its existence the Dukes of Urbino survived the Papal
struggle for temporal power, and Italy was a
prey to the foreigner, who made it the battle-
field of nations, and who would readily have
seized on any attempt of the Popes to extend
their power as an opportunity to deprive them
of what they already possessed.

Thus we see that San Marino owes its existence not so much to its own integrity, as to the
happy run of circumstances, which so enabled
it to carry on the method of government which
suited its inhabitants—a race of peasants,
who liked to till the ground and grow their
grapes without the interference of a foreign
despot.

The liberty of San Marino has been most
extolled by Melchiore Delfico, who indeed so
eulogises this little State as to leave an impres-
sion that here has existed for centuries a society
of gods in disguise ; never for a day have they
swerved from their upright course, no vicious

symptoms have here ever arisen, and perfection
on earth is the echo of his work; whereas on
the other hand, Carlo Fea, who writes to assert
the dominion of the Holy See over this little
people, vituperates this author and treats the
Republic as a thing of nought, and its inhabitants as dangerous upstarts, who dare to unfurl
the flag of liberty under the very eyes of
the Papal See. He alleges case after case
of acts of subserviency which no free-minded
people would ever have performed, but bases
all his arguments for Papal supremacy on the
dangerous quagmires of the Pepinian and other
donations; whilst he sums up by saying, 'The
Republic owes its preservation more than anything else to the attachment of its inhabitants
to their Saint, to the locality, to the form of
government, which binds and obliges everyone,
and to the pleasing and exalted idea of ancient
liberty which under any other government
would long ago have perished.'[1] He extols
the leniency of the Popes in allowing them to

[1] Carlo Fea, 'Diritto sovrano della santa sede sul Comacchio
e la Repubblica di San Marino.'

continue under their own government, forget-
ting to allege at the same time any reasons
which obliged the Popes to do so. Clement
XII., who regranted them their liberty after
Alberoni's occupation, was led to do so, knowing that by this he could avoid an appeal to
any other power, for Austria would only have
been too glad of a foothold in the States of the
Church, and Alberoni was always on the look-
out for means to embroil Europe in another
war.   *GOA comporuso* —

In short, the existence of San Marino forms
a good point from which to survey the history
of Italy in general. Weak of itself and unable
to raise a finger against a foreign foe, it has
gone along with the times, an idiosyncrasy
which could not have existed in any other
country but in Italy, and which modern constitutional Italy has left untouched, inasmuch as
our Republic has arguments now to adduce
in behalf of its liberty which would make it
hard for a Government, based on modern constitutional principles, to touch it.

The whole spirit of San Marino's history

and character is embodied in a simple tale of
some centuries ago, without date, but told as a
story of the past, by an historian[1] who wrote a
short but faithful account of San Marino, about
a hundred years ago. Envious of the tran-
quillity which reigned on Mount Titanus, certain people repaired thither, anxious to throw
in their lot with the peaceful inhabitants of
our rock. Their petition was presented at a
Council, and some of the Councillors were
inclined towards receiving it, when one high in
authority amongst them, being alarmed at the
specious offers of the petitioners to bring certain benefices to the State, and at the astute
arguments adduced, ordered the envoy to
appear in Council, and spoke as follows : ' Of
a truth your propositions sound well ; but know
that we are a somewhat matter-of-fact people,
and all we require is to know how to govern
our small community, whilst ye are people of
the Court, and know all the cunning of the
outer world ; we wish for nothing new, that ye
need share your brains with us.' The Coun-

---

[1] Linda.

cillors echoed the sentiments of their leader,
and the envoy was not allowed to respond,
whilst those who had wished to accept the offer
never suffered their names to transpire for very
shame. Thus it was, and thus it still is with
the people of San Marino; without mingling
with the outer world they have retained their
simplicity and customs, and at the same time
they have unconsciously retained a living
museum, so to speak, of mediæval Italian life.

A Russian Prince, Beloselky by name, a
fervent friend of letters, and an intimate of
Voltaire's and Rousseau's, once wrote a curious
poem to the Sammarinesi, a strange mixture of
prose and burlesque verses. After congratu-
lating them on the happy termination of the
Alberoni affair, he gives them some humorous
advice, prefaced by the following questionable
compliment:

> Vous n'avez pas l'éclat que donne la victoire,
> Mais votre état fleurit depuis treize cents ans.

Nevertheless the Sammarinesi are very
proud of it, and consider that their long period
of freedom compensates in every way for the

lack of martial honours. A curious story of
the sixteenth century, however, shows us that
the Sammarinesi are not altogether without
their laurels; for a war indeed they had, and
that against a party of gipsies. As the story
savours of a romance, and lacks the authenticity
of history, I here give it as it stands, and it
may be taken for what it is worth.

In or about the year 1556, a young bookseller, Francesco Ballero by name, established
himself in a shop in the market-place of San
Marino. As he fulfilled all his duties to Church
and State in a thoroughly orthodox manner
no one enquired of him from whence he came,
complaining only of his great reticence, and
that he never was to be found elsewhere than
in his shop or at church, and if perchance he
took a walk when the church bells were not
ringing he chose the most lonely paths and
slopes of Mount Titanus. Three years passed
thus, when one Sabbath evening he came in
great haste to the dwelling of the parish priest,
to tell him that the town was in the greatest
danger. The aged divine shook his hoary

locks, and said, 'You dream, my son, how could our peaceful little town be in danger?'

'From some gipsies, father,' said Francesco, 'who threaten to bring a sickness on the town.'

'You must be very clever,' rejoined the priest, 'for no one can understand their language but one of themselves.'

'But suppose I am one of them myself,' mysteriously added the bookseller, and went on to relate how that when he was a student at Bologna he had been seized with a desire to visit the whole of Italy, and in his travels found himself one day at Naples. Here he chanced to see a gipsy girl dancing on the Chiaja, dressed more gaily than her comrades, and of a beauty which captivated the hearts of all the young Neapolitans, but she steadfastly refused all the money, jewels, and flattery heaped on her by her admirers. Nevertheless she condescended to accept a bouquet or two silently offered her by the amorous Ballero, and the dark brown eyes of the lovely Drakh or Vine, as she was called, burnt deep into his heart. On learning that the troop had moved away one day he determined to follow them and declare his love. At the wayside inn close to where the gipsies were encamped he was warned against their robberies and acts of barbarity; but his love conquered all his fears, and nothing daunted he plunged into the forest on his horse. After riding for two hours he came across the first members of the band, looking very different from what they did in their gay clothes at Naples. They were dressed in the vilest rags, and looked regular ruffians. In no way dismayed, he rode on to the centre of their encampment, where he was soon surrounded and dragged off his horse. They stripped him to his shirt, and were preparing to hang him to a tree, when a cry for help announced his quandary to Drakh, who at once ordered him to be let loose and his property to be restored to him. Her unruly subjects, for Drakh was no other than their Queen, at first refused to allow their prey to escape; but she disarmed the ringleader, and, to the surprise of all, announced Francesco as her husband. When released from the tree, Drakh and Francesco drank water together out of the same vessel, and ate together a piece of bread, and thus they became man and wife after the customs of this nomad race.

The aged priest now felt assured that Ballero was mad, and asked him how he managed to escape from the horde.

'By flight, reverend father,' he replied, 'when I heard they were about to set out for Africa.'

'You did well, young man,' rejoined the priest. 'Here in San Marino you are quite safe from the "Vine" and her rabble. Go, say some half-dozen paternosters, to ease your mind.'

'You are mistaken, father,' replied Francesco. 'I beseech you to hearken to my words; for I saw a portion of Drakh's band, and they are prepared to poison the wells of the town.'

The priest, however, convinced that the bookseller was mad, paid no heed to this warning, and neglected to inform the Council of what he had heard.

Francesco Ballero forthwith left the town to discover what he could, and try to save the inhabitants from their predicted doom; but it was too late. Two days after his interview with the priest a terrible sickness broke out, and great was the priest's remorse at having neglected the warning. In a few days half the inhabitants fell a sacrifice to this terrible scourge, whilst many more were dangerously ill.

When Ballero returned to the town the greatest attention was paid to all he had to say. He warned them that the gipsies now considered the town sufficiently exhausted, and purposed falling upon it and plundering it the next day.

In great dismay the Councillors assembled, and ordered the criers to go round and summon all those capable of bearing arms, and only about two hundred could answer the call. However, so enraged were they at the treachery which threatened them, that they solemnly swore to avenge themselves on the brown tribe, and not to spare even the women or children— not one of the murderers of their families should be allowed to escape.

It was resolved to leave all the gates wide open, and to wait in ambush the approach of

the invaders. Half of the next day was spent
in terrible suspense by the inhabitants of our
rock, when suddenly in rushed a motley group
of men, women, and children, all armed, and
their eyes gleaming with fury and cruelty. The
Sammarinesi rushed out upon them with shouts
of defiance, hewing and piercing right and left,
sparing, as they had sworn, neither age nor sex,
the more so as the small brown children used
their daggers with a dexterity beyond their
age. After a sharp struggle, victory declared
itself on the side of the Republicans, and the
piazza and surrounding streets were strewn with
the dead bodies of the slain, whilst only a small
handful of gipsies escaped to tell their tale.
None of the brave burghers were killed, and
Francesco Ballero alone was missing, nor was he
again seen or heard of. It was said that he had
been seen fighting against the gipsies, and that
he had been surrounded by them, a tall, dark
woman standing by giving them orders. When
all further search proved in vain, and no hope
of seeing him again was entertained, his shop
was opened, and his papers were examined.

Therein a will was found, taking an eternal farewell of San Marino, and leaving to the town all his worldly goods, with which, so runs the story, an orphanage was to be founded. But this story of Francesco Ballero and his orphanage is looked upon by the Sammarinesi as far more mythical than the legends of their Saint. Of a truth, at Serravalle, an orphanage does exist; but though the endowment thereof is shrouded in obscurity, they do not recognise this foreigner in any way as their benefactor.

CHAPTER XIII.

CONSTITUTIONAL SKETCHES.

*Les coutumes d'un peuple esclave sont une partie de sa servitude, et celles d'un peuple libre sont une partie de sa liberté.—*Montesquieu, *Esprit des Lois.*

THE early government of the few inhabitants which were gathered round the sanctuary of Marinus corresponds in most respects to that in vogue amongst all primitive societies. The family was here considered the basis of all political representation, as amongst our own Anglo-Saxon ancestors. Each family deputed its head to vote and superintend its interests in the '*Arringo*,' which was the ' patron absolute.' By this matters political and judicial were decided, the wicked were punished, and from this the good received their reward.

With the advance of time, however, the in-convenience of such large and unwieldy assem-

blies was felt here as elsewhere. Towards the
close of the fourteenth century the authority of
the Arringo was placed in the hands of a
Council of sixty, which is still the governing
power of the State. Nevertheless, the right of
the Arringo to assemble was reserved, and it
always meets twice a year, a few days after the
installation of the Captains. But this assembly
exists now merely in name, for the thirty or
forty heads of families who collect on these
occasions to witness the presentation of two or
three petitions to the newly-appointed Captains has but little resemblance to that which
at one time entirely controlled the affairs of
State. No penalty is now imposed on absen-
tees, the fine of one penny having fallen into
disuse ; and it is now only used as a medium
for presenting requests which the Council may
grant or refuse as they like. On one occasion
on which I happened to be present, a petition for the establishment of telegraphic communication was duly presented and read, and
two others for the extension of certain road
works, the entire ceremony lasting only about

twenty minutes, and the petitions being put
aside for discussion by the Council at some
future period. Hence it is obvious that to the
Council of sixty we must look as the only
executive power.

Great is the diversity of opinion expressed
by various authors as to the nature of the
government of San Marino. We find Cima-
relli calling it a 'monarchical society,' Matteo
Valli and Delfico style it a 'democratic government,' and Auger St. Hippolyte looks upon it as
an 'isonomia,' or equality of rights ; whilst[1]
Addison holds it to be an 'oligarchy.' But let us
look more closely into the constitution of this
Council of sixty before we make our decision.

When the Arringo relinquished its rights
into the hands of sixty of its members, it abandoned its executive power entirely; for the
members of this Council when once elected
were to remain so for life, and on the death of
one of the members the Council itself elects
another in his place. Thus Addison was cor-
rect in calling it an oligarchy.

[1] Addison's *Travels in Italy.*

But to go a step farther, whether by custom, statute, or recognised consent, this body is divided into three estates, twenty members being noble, twenty citizens or inhabitants of the Città and Borgo, and twenty country people or landowners; whereas Addison tells us that half are noble and half citizens, which could not be the case, as the number of noble families in San Marino never reached thirty. Thus it will appear that the government of San Marino is a well-balanced oligarchy; the nobles themselves owing their election to the Council, and, being in so small a minority, have no extensive power.

When a vacancy occurs, each member, beginning with the Captains, proposes a candidate, and each candidate proposed is ballotted for, and each of the three estates has full right to vote at the election of a member of another.

Members of this Council must be over twenty-five years of age; a son cannot be a member during the lifetime of his father, nor more than one of any number of brothers who live together.

The dangerous elements of an oligarchy have never had full play in San Marino, for the sixty only represent 1,243 hearths, so there can be but little room for any unconstitutional proceedings. However, we have seen in these pages that irregularities began to creep in towards the middle of the sixteenth century. At that time the number rose to eighty, and was afterwards again reduced to sixty ; and in the next century, so great was the constitutional languor, it was reduced to forty-five, and in 1739, when Alberoni came, there were only twenty-three. Hence, we can see no perfect constitution here—no Utopia, as many French Republican writers would make us believe.

For the assembly of the Council an order of one of the Captains is required, and the bell of the castle must be rung, and the town-crier proclaims it in all the streets. Their proceedings are conducted in strict privacy, none but Councillors being admitted to the room, nor may they afterwards divulge the subjects of their deliberations. Besides this, the office is tantamount to hereditary; for if there be no positive objection to a son, he is invariably elected a Councillor in his deceased father's stead.

Out of this Council of sixty, a body of twelve is chosen, and forms an 'Economic Council,' as the statute describes it, to act as an intermediate body between the Great Council and the Captains; and their office is to direct matters financial, public instruction, agriculture, &c., to which the Great Council has given its consent. Two-thirds of this Council of twelve are renewed every year, sixteen candidates being proposed, one-half citizens and one-half countrymen, from which the ballot is to select the requisite eight.

The Council of sixty is comprehensively termed 'The Prince of San Marino,' and to exercise their power they elect a Duumvirate twice every year, and these two magistrates are called the Captains; their power is simply derivative, the public money is not even entrusted to their care, but is left in the hands of the Camerlengo, or Treasurer. One Captain is always noble, and the other either a citizen or a countryman, and their power is indivisible, except that through etiquette the nobleman keeps the keys and seals and has a certain priority in matters of form. Hence, selected as they are from both classes of society, one is always a check on the actions of the other.

To be eligible for the Captaincy a man must be over twenty-five years of age, and a native of San Marino; therefore Sammarinesi living abroad generally contrive to return home, that their children may first see the light of day on this mountain. Again, he must be free from any disgrace or judicial infamy, and, lastly, he must not have been elected Captain within the last three years.

The oath which they take on assuming office binds them to keep the statutes which provide for the summoning of Council every week, and for the entire subserviency of the Captains to that Council. It runs as follows:—

'We *N.* and *M.*, Captain and Defender of the Castle of San Marino, swear to rule and govern for the next six months to come from this day the said Castle of San Marino and its villages, with the men and other things pertaining to the said Castle and its Court, with all our power; and we will keep, and cause to be kept, the Statutes and Ordinances written in this Book to the honour and majesty of the said Castle of San Marino, and we will protect its goods from all treachery, and we will observe all these things with good faith and without fraud. So help us, God.'

In ancient times the Priest or Abbot of San Marino used to carry out the dictates of the Arringo, probably the successors of Saint Marinus himself, as heads of the ecclesiastical establishment continued to act as Regents. But in 1244 we find two Consuls treating with the Feltrian Bishop, Ugolino. This name continued in vogue for some time in San Marino, in common with other Italian States at that period, and it was not till early in the fourteenth century that we find the statutes speaking of the Captain and the Defender. But the second name was soon abandond in ordinary parlance;

and with some few exceptions, the Duumvirate
have been styled Captains ever since.

With the growing intensity in epithets
common to the rest of Italy, the modest Signori
Capitani of the fourteenth century are now
addressed as ' L'eccellentissima Regenza.'

During the course of their history we find
several anomalies in their election, especially
during times of the great social decay, when
the legal age of two citizens had to be set aside
in 1639 in default of other citizens to fill the
post. But taken as a whole, the durability of
the system, and the tenacity with which the
Sammarinesi have stuck to their constitution,
can find no parallel in history. No Captain
has ever tried to assume more than his just
power, or in any way to tyrannise, or to be-
tray his country into the hands of those who
would amply have rewarded him, nor is one
single Captain's name mentioned with contumely.

The mode in which the Captains are chosen
is decidedly intricate. Twice a year, on March
15 and September 15, those who are to assume

the post of Regents for the coming term are
chosen as follows: Twelve electors are taken
by lot from the members of the Council, and
each proposes a candidate for the Regency from
among his fellow Councillors. Upon this the
names of six of these, chosen by the majority of
the whole Council, are written upon three lots,
it having been duly arranged that one noble
and one of the other two estates be placed
together. These preliminaries having been
completed, the whole Council go in great pomp,
accompanied by music and soldiers, to the
parish church towards the evening of the day
on which the election takes place, their atten-
dants carrying torches to add to the solemnity
of the scene.

Here the parish priest is in attendance, and
having read aloud the names on the three lots,
encloses them in three ballot balls, and puts
them into a silver urn, shakes it well, and then,
in the presence of the assembled multitude, a
little boy of about eight years old extracts one
of the lots which contains the names of the
Captains elect.

Then, amidst the peals of the organ, the priest reads aloud the result, and the populace respond with loud applause, recognising in this ceremony the voice of the oracle which proclaims to them their new '*Preposti*' for the coming six months.

Elected in this way a fortnight before, the new Captains await the first of the coming month for their entrance into office. This festival is attended with all the pomp and panoply that San Marino can muster; visitors come from afar, few indeed in number, but enough for the accommodation afforded them. The brilliant flag of the Republic, all blue and white silk with the arms of the State emblazoned thereon, is unfurled from the Sala dell' Udienza, and the Pianello, with its enchanting view over the Umbrian mountains, assumes quite a holiday appearance.

An army of twenty-eight strong, in the gay blue uniform of the Republic, with a band of considerable power for noise if not for music, is in readiness to escort the newly-appointed functionaries to attend Mass in the parish

church of San Marino, previous to their taking
the oath and their final installation as Regents.
Early in the morning they are saluted in their
own houses by their fellow-citizens, and afterwards confer with the outgoing Captains in the
Sala del Commune.

The dress of the Captains is striking and
handsome ; a black silk *juste-au-corps*, and
puffed trunk hose, black silk stockings, a large
circular cloak of black velvet lined with blue
silk, fastened with gold cords and aiguillettes
hanging down one side, and a white cravat
with long ends fringed with lace. Six of these
suits are kept in store to be ready for any
emergency in the size of Captains. The badge
of office, which is eventually to be transferred,
being still in possession of the outgoing Captains,
consists of the grand cordon of the Equestrian
Order of San Marino.[1] A broad blue and white
ribbon passed through the jewel, which hangs
low upon the breast, is plaited so as to form a
full ruff or collar behind. Their caps of black
velvet, bound with ermine, are never donned.

[1] *Vide* chapter xiv.

but carried by grand lackeys, called Donzelli,
six in number, one of whom is always in
attendance on the Captains. They look like
gaudy London footmen, in blue livery with
silver facings, and on their backs three upright
points of silver lace, to represent the three
peaks of the Republic.

On an occasion when I had the good fortune
to witness this ceremony, the gay and imposing
procession wound its way upwards to the parish
church, the musicians and soldiers forming a
double line down the nave for the officials to
pass through, the former enlivening the scene
with gay music, more calculated to inspire
the minds of the audience with feelings of
hilarity than to endue them with the solemnity
of the proceedings. Such, indeed, was the case,
as most of the spectators took the opportunity
of chatting with their friends who had come
from a distance.

Installed on a tribune of crimson brocade
backed by the Republican arms, to the left of
the altar, the two Captains sat side by side,
and together looked every inch a king, whilst

their modest successors took a humble place lower down the Church, looking slightly awe-stricken at the glory that was to come upon them.

When the formalities of the Mass were concluded, the officials and as many of the spectators as could be accommodated in the Sala del Consiglio, well suited to the size of the Republic, repaired thither to hear the discourse and witness the taking of the oath.

To a stranger anxious to acquire information about the Republic the "*discorso*" was of high interest, but to those accustomed to hear the same eulogy and injunctions twice every year it must have been extremely wearisome.

The audience were taken back to far distant ages when St. Marinus founded this ever free family upon this impregnable rock; they were informed of the kindness of the neighbouring Dukes of Urbino and treachery of the Malatesti of Rimini, and no kindly words were spoken about Alberoni and his occupation; Victor Emmanuel, Napoleon I., and Garibaldi, were all politely alluded to; and, in conclusion, dire

R

punishments were promised to the wicked who might scheme against San Marino's perpetual liberty; and injunctions were given to the incoming Captains to maintain the laws, and to look after the instruction of youth, as a primary element in the well-being of the State.

At the conclusion of this harangue a Donzello read the customary oath to the incoming Captains, who swore by placing their hands on the book containing the same. The outgoing Captains then transferred the badge of office from their own necks to those of the new ones, and resigned their places on the throne to them. The new but timorous-looking Regents received the respectful bows of the ex-monarchs, who then vanished by a side-door. After having received the keys of the various departments of state, the seals, &c., which are put into a handsome casket, the ceremony was concluded.

The Captains always leave home '*incogniti*,' and one of them may stay away a week or more if he can so arrange matters with the Council; and a citizen of San Marino, who may chance to meet a Captain abroad always treats him as '*incognito*,' whereas at home he would address him as '*eccellenza*'

When attending Council, and when busy in the affairs of State, the Captains are always attended by a Donzello, but on these occasions they dispense with the magnificent apparel of State, and wear a suit of evening clothes; these also are kept in stock, and are not always the best of fits.

The offices held by the Sammarinesi are but slightly remunerative, for the Captain receives only a trifling monthly salary, whereas an ambassador of the Republic, besides his travelling expenses and remuneration for loss of time, is only by the Statute entitled to tenpence a day. The Captains have, however, the monopoly of salt during their term of office.

They are obliged, at least once during their six months of office, to visit the three Castles of Serravalle, Mongiardino, and Faetano, and to see that all is proceeding satisfactorily within the town. Without the leave of the Council they may not spend more than thirty francs on any public building, nor may they place their name or arms on anything built during their regency.

On entering into office the Captains select a Secretary of State and a Secretary of Finance, who also receive a slight salary, and remain in office for the same time. The financial affairs of San Marino would form a model for any Chancellor of any Exchequer; they not only possess no public debt, but have a considerable balance at their bankers in Florence. In fact, enterprise is not one of the gifts of their many rulers; their expenses are next to nothing, and their taxes the same. So they manage to live contented, but always stationary, with a population not perceptibly increasing. Nevertheless, many energetic undertakings have been carried out in the way of roads and improving the streets of the capital ; also education has been made compulsory, and hence an attendant expense on the Government.

The following is an average specimen of a Sammarinese budget (1865–1872) :—

Receipts.

Lire.

	Lire.
From dues	52,000
From taxes . . .	53,900
Divers products . . .	6,600

Lire 112,500 = £4,500

Expenses.

Lire.

	Lire.
To Regency . . .	8,200
Justice	8,200
Army	8,500
Administration and finance .	11,500
Health	7,700
Agriculture . . .	2,000
Public works . . .	38,000
Industry, commerce and post	2,800
Public instruction . .	17,100
Charity	5,000

Lire 109,000 = £4,384

In accordance with a convention with United Italy[1] San Marino now coins its own money, which is good in both countries; but its coins exist more in name than in anything else, for the pieces of ' one *soldo*,' dating from 1864, and of ' two *soldi*,' dating from 1875, are but rarely found in circulation, and only two specimens of ' five *lire* ' pieces were struck, and these now adorn the numismatic collection in the museum.

[1] *Vide* chapter xi.

Stamps, however, with the Republican arms upon them, are always used for letters leaving the State ; and of these the Sammarinesi are not a little proud, for a few sheets of each kind were framed, and sent to the Paris Exhibition of 1878, and are also to be seen on the walls of the picture-gallery in the museum.

As the above-mentioned convention with Italy shows the exact position in which San Marino stands with the ruling power of the country in which it is engulfed, and the exact extent of the liberty recognised, it will be well to give a slight epitome of the same.[1]

'The most serene Republic of San Marino, and Victor Emmanuel, King of Italy, recognising the reciprocal convenience of introducing some modifications with regard to a former treaty (namely, that of 1862), through the aid of their respective ambassadors, draw up the following articles,' dated March 27, 1872. All judicial sentences, public Acts, condemnations, &c., passed in either of the two States, shall

---

[1] 'Convenzione di buon vicinato e di amicizia conchiusa il 27 Marzo, 1872, a Firenze.'

hold good in the other, according to the customs of procedure in the respective jurisdictions, and citizens of either may demand the legal assistance of both countries, provided that they have conformed to the laws in use in the place where the assistance is demanded.

Cases in which extradition can be demanded are drawn up in full length, and include every misdemeanour of which mankind is capable; and the extradition is to be put into execution immediately on the production of the writ, with which is abolished the freedom for three days formerly granted to all malefactors who entered the confines of the Republic; but a ten years' sojourn in either State will prevent the extradition being demanded.

If a soldier of either State deserts to the other, he is to be sent back with his horse, and all his accoutrements.

Passports between the two countries are considered unnecessary, and money coined in either is valid in both. Instead of a customhouse between the two countries, the kingdom of Italy gives up a portion of the revenue arising from the custom duties, proportioned to the number of San Marino's inhabitants, kindly calculated at 9,000.

Patents of all kinds granted by the kingdom of Italy are to be respected by San Marino, and the Republic covenants not to set up a printing-press in its territories, to avoid any difficulty about copyrights.

Tobacco is not to be grown within the Republic's territories, and the kingdom of Italy hands over annually at cost price 78,000 kilograms of white salt from Cervia, and 70,000 kilograms of foreign tobacco; and in case of need a further supply will also be given at cost price.

After discussing these and a few minor points, the most serene Republic being confidently assured that its privileges and liberties will be ever respected by the King, pledges itself never to accept the protection of any other power. On the execution of this treaty, Victor Emmanuel presented the Republic with a bronze medallion of himself, which is kept in the palace of the regency.

An Italian Consul resides in the old palazzo where Count Borghese lived, whilst the Republic has a deputy at Rome, to watch over its interests at head-quarters.

Several minor officials superintend minor offices in the State, and are likewise elected by the Council of Sixty. The two doctors form no unimportant part in the domestic economy of San Marino. They are under Government pay, and are obliged to kill or cure free of charge. Likewise the schoolmaster is a great person, whose duty it is to teach all the youthful Republicans, and now that education is compulsory his office is no sinecure. With a wholesome modesty, the Sammarinesi have ordained that the two doctors and the schoolmaster must always be foreigners, recognising the evil effects of continually choosing such important personages out of so restricted a population, whose abilities are not amongst their most prominent points.

Conservators are appointed for preserving all public edifices, for overlooking the cleanliness of the streets, who, by the way, effect

their duties far from efficiently; and where drain-
age could be perfect and at the least expense,
we are surprised to find an entire absence of
it.   Again, the custody of the clock in the
Pianello is another important office in the gift
of the Council.   In the next chapter we will
discuss their judicial arrangements, and some
other points of internal economy.

CHAPTER XIV.

INTERNAL ECONOMY.

A così riposato, a così bello
Viver di cittadini, a così fida
Cittadinanza, a così dolce ostello.—DANTE.

No part of San Marino's internal economy brings us more forcibly face to face with Italy of the past than the existence of a foreign *Podestà*, to superintend their legal arrangements.

In mediæval Florence, for example, the foreign element which was introduced into the State not only superintended the course of justice, but also commanded one of the most noble battalions of the army; whilst at Milan, where the family feuds of the Torriani and Visconti constantly plunged the State into civil war, and in all other Republics, so great was the party spirit, that one side could not trust a legal representative of the other to administer justice impartially. In this small mountain Republic—the *débris* of Italian liberty, as it has been termed—we still find this custom in vogue ; and centuries after the *Bargello* of Florence has ceased to open its gates to a foreign judge, we here recognise customs as immutable as the rock on which they have been engendered.

The early statutory arrangements of San Marino are closely interwoven with those of the Duchy of Urbino, though so far back as 1253 we find mention made of statutes, and again, in 1278, to check the inhabitants from commercial intercourse with the neighbouring town of Corena, and from time to time we are told that the Sammarinesi availed themselves of a time of peace to revise the same. Yet in all matters of weighty importance the inhabitants of our rock seem to have been in the habit of paying a small annual sum to have the benefit of the advice of the neighbouring Podestà of Montefeltro. Whereas, in 1367, when Carlo Peruzzi made strenuous endeavours to get all Romagna into his grasp, the Sammarinesi, to

prevent further disturbances in their rights,
sought the aid of a judge from Rimini, Franceschino by name, well skilled in law, to decide
the weighty point of their liberty; and about
this time, such was the spirit for legal exactness
kindled in their breasts, that by order of the
Council their Captains and five reformers set to
work to compile a new code, which, under the
title of ' *The Statutes of the Commune of the
Castle of San Marino,*' appears as the first authentic copy of these laws, which, we are told,
the saintly Marinus first compiled, and handed
down to his successors.

Various alterations and amendments during
the course of the next two centuries were added
to this work, to suit the emergencies of the
times; but in 1592, owing to the 'laceration
and consumption of the book,' the result of the
turbulence of the times, the Grand Council
found it necessary to appoint eight revisers,
who, with the Captains, sat day by day poring
over their arduous task of compiling a new
code. So long, however, were these functionaries in producing the necessary work that the

course of justice was sorely impeded, and recourse had to be made to a private copy of the
laws, compiled by and in the hands of the
Bonelli family, which continued to be used till
the year 1600, when, by dint of strenuous exertions, a new code was compiled and printed,
and forms the basis of that which is now in use ;
but at the time it gave so little satisfaction to
the community at large, owing to the barbarity
of some of its penalties, that in 1602 there was
much talk of revising it, and in 1621 the
Council went so far as to appoint revisers ; but
this was never done, and the code has simply
gone through a refining process, as circumstances occurred.

During all this period their kind friends, the
Dukes of Urbino, continued to impress on the
inhabitants of Mount Titanus the necessity of
appointing some foreign commissary to superintend their courts of law ; but the Captains continued to plead poverty, and preferred to pay
the customary trifling sum for the use of anyone
the Duke might send them, from time to time,
to act as Podestà, and decide in all cases of im-

portance, to having a regular paid lawyer of their own.

However, this personage sent by the Duke came so seldom, and it was so precarious a reed on which to trust when the Duke himself was in difficulties, that the force of circumstances obliged the appointment of a commissary by the State to direct the course of law, who, in the year 1600, became a definite and essential element in the constitution.

He was delegated by the Regency, and took oaths to be subservient to the same, and to decide impartially in all cases, civil and criminal; but his decisions were not to be final, for the Council reserved to itself the power of a veto, and appointed two judges from amongst their own body to whom appeals might be made, whilst the decision of the Council of Twelve alone was held to be final. At the present time this foreign commissary is obliged to be a doctor of law, who has graduated at a legal university, and whose reputation for legal learning is irreproachable.

In 1834 a new edition of the laws was

published, short indeed, and crude, but leaving
no loophole for the inhabitants to cast off their
long-established reputation for honesty, probity,
and morality. A preface thereto speaks in flowing
terms of the antiquity of the Republic and its
laws, how these date from the thirteenth century, and have only been amended from time to
time to suit emergencies, and how, thanks to
these, San Marino is the sole survivor of Italian
freedom. With regard to the transmission of
property, tutelage of minors, dower, &c., the
laws are entirely based on the old Roman codes,
and offer no novelty to the student of Justinian;
but, in turning to the minor points of detail,
one is confronted with many idiosyncrasies.
Amongst other State officials we find regulations for electing the schoolmasters and doctors, who must be foreigners, in the following
manner: the Council have the option of fixing
on any number of electors they may think
necessary, who are then chosen by lot, and it is
their duty then to fix on anyone fitted to occupy
either of these posts, the Council always retaining its power of vetoing the appointment if

against their wishes. Dire are the punishments denounced by the Statutes on anyone who should attempt any conspiracy, or suggest to give the government over into the hands of a neighbouring State. Any Captains who may refuse to fill the office when elected are likewise to be treated as traitors, unless they can allege any valid excuse. All games of chance are strictly forbidden, and certain regulations against swearing appear to us a little strong if carried out to the letter. Every man who takes in vain any sacred name, San Marino and the Blessed Virgin being placed in the same category, and the other saints in a descending scale, according to their respective merits, is to be heavily fined; but whosoever shall strike the images of the same, whether with wood, iron, stone, and the like, is to have his hand cut off; but a heavy fine for the inferior saints, even in this case, is deemed sufficient.

So jealous are the Sammarinesi of their character, so susceptible are they of any adverse criticism by their neighbours, that at the end of the last century, when a Riminese of the name

of Bava, on one occasion spoke of the Republic
as a refuge for thieves and robbers, bankrupt
traders, and vagabonds, and when this speech
was reported to the Council of Sixty, they forthwith passed a law, so runs the story, that this
man and all his relations, and all who bore his
name, should be excluded for ever from the
Republican territories. Thirty years afterwards
a man and woman, on a stormy night, applied
for shelter in Serravalle. The man unfortunately
addressed the woman as ' Signora Bava,' whereupon the peasant started up and exclaimed,
' Away from my house, every one with the
name of Bava,' and the unfortunate female was
turned out into the cold and rain.

No one is prouder of an acquired reputation
for justice than a Sammarinese. This little
Republic stands exceedingly high in its own
estimation, nor is this pride calculated to be
diminished by the many flattering eulogies and
terms of respect by which it has been addressed
by various potentates. Louis Philippe, of France,
on the occasion of his being enrolled amongst
their patricians, wrote them a truly fulsome

letter, addressed to his ' Chers et bons amis,'
whilst the Emperor Ferdinand of Austria styled
them his ' Beloved and respectable friends.' On
the other hand, what must have been the feelings of a haughty Doge of the proud Republic
of Venice on receiving a letter from the poor
inhabitants of this isolated rock, addressed ' To
our very Dear Sister, the Most Serene Republic
of Venice.'

No Sammarinese is ignorant of a story which
is told, contrasting their uprightness in a most
favourable light with that of Venice, and which
runs as follows: A Venetian merchant, who
was once owed some sum of money by a Sammarinese, as the best means of recovering his debt,
repaired in person to the Republic, and went
straight to one of the Captains of the time,
whom he found treading grapes in his vineyard.
Much staggered at this, after the grandeur and
pomp of his own dignitaries, he half repented
him of his journey, and the trouble he had
taken; nevertheless, he went to the Captain, and
told his story. This functionary thereupon left
his employment, and sent for the delinquent

with all haste, who acknowledged the debt without hesitation.   Orders were immediately given
for the selling of his house and worldly goods,
whereupon the money was soon forthcoming, as
the debtor was by no means so poor as would
have appeared from his shortcomings, and the
Venetian went home rejoicing, and profound in
his respect for our Republic.   Some time afterwards the same creditor having occasion to sue
a debtor in the court of Venice, and having
experienced the law's delays, and its glorious
uncertainty, gave vent to this expression, which
at San Marino has almost passed into a proverb,
' A simple grape-treader of San Marino is worth
far more than ten big-wigs of Venice.'

Of late years, after the abolition of gaming-
tables in other countries, some few were to be
found in the Borgo, but they were always stre-
nuously opposed by the Government, and when
some foreign speculators went so far as to offer
to build grand hotels, open a railway and
gambling-houses at San Marino, the Council
refused, worthy successors of those who set on
one side the offer made by Napoleon ; though

some of the Councillors, whether through the
advantages they expected the Republic would
reap from becoming a second Monte Carlo, or
through bribes of the speculators, which we are
told were offered but never taken, voted in its
favour, but were silenced by an overwhelming
majority. Now, as we have seen, gambling of
all kinds is forbidden by the laws, and the Sammarinesi rest contented with their modest games
of *écarté* with no stakes thereon.

The military force of San Marino is somewhat under 2,000 strong; half the able-bodied
men of every family must be enrolled in the
army between the ages of sixteen and fifty-five,
except they happen to be government officers,
doctors, priests, and students. The first corps
is called the ' *Guardia della Reggenza*,' detach-
ments of which serve as an escort of honour to
the Regents, and are stationed at the ' Palazzo
Communale ' during audiences, and the sittings
of the Council. Their uniform is very gaudy,
blue with yellow facings, which in some way
makes up for their want of soldier-like appearance in other respects. The second corps is

called the ' *Guardia della Rocca*,' whose uniform
is blue with red facings. Two companies,
called respectively '*Granatieri*' and '*Cacciatori*,'
are dispersed through the city, Borgo, and
Castles, and are ready, on the slightest notice,
to turn their hands to anything; they assist at
feasts, act as policemen on emergencies, and
follow their various avocations when not required. Their uniform was once blue with white
facings, but these are unfortunately now worn
out, and so peacefully inclined is the Government that they have not thought it necessary to
go to the expense of replacing them with new
ones.

The residue of the armed force is scattered
throughout the country, and in no way differ
from the rest of the community, except that
it is obligatory for them to possess a gun and
ammunition, and a cockade, against emergencies,
which accounts for the fact that so many indulge
themselves in field sports; and on a Sunday's
festa most of the male population carry a gun
with them, which proves at least their love of
the chase, though, judging from the spare

amount of game to be seen about, their chances
of a good day's sport are but small; indeed they
only profess to go in search of chaffinches, and
other small fry, to form a delicacy for their
tables, and when the bird betrays itself by a
song, they lie in wait under a tree until an
opportunity is afforded for shooting at it as it is
seated on a bough.   In short, the Sammarinesi
are not a bellicose race, and have enjoyed an
immunity from war longer than most countries,
and since they fought under their own banner
for the Dukes of Urbino, their military prowess
has never had an opportunity of showing itself,
unless we accept as true the story of the
gipsies.

The agrarian system in vogue at San Marino
is the *mezzeria*, or metuary system, by which half
the yearly profits go to the tenant, and half to the
landlord, in lieu of rent, the evil effects of which
are felt here as elsewhere in Italy.   But the taxes
are extremely light, being only one-twentieth
part of those paid by the Italian landowners
across the border, the moral of their rulers
being that propounded by one of their own

economists, that 'a great part of liberty consists in paying little.'

The three castles of Serravalle, Faetano, and Mongiardino have their separate syndics, the

CASTLE OF SERRAVALLE.

first having six Councillors, the second four, and the third two Vice-Captains, who render an account of their proceedings to the Captains and treasurer at head-quarters. Officials to superintend the affairs of the smaller hamlets are taken by lot out of the Council of Sixty, and their names are proclaimed aloud at the '*Arringo*' after the installation of the Captains in office.

After the capital, the town of Serravalle offers the only point of interest to the anti-quarian. Here a handsome old portal, and the remnants of walls, point out an old stronghold of the Malatesti before they were subjugated by Pius II. and his alliance, and their territories meted out to their neighbours. This castle was shattered by an earthquake some few years ago, but still forms a conspicuous object for the surrounding country.

In the church of Serravalle, on either side of the altar, the visitor is greeted by statues of two old friends; Gaudentius, Bishop of Rimini, who made Marinus his deacon, stands in a niche on the left, with a cynical expression of coun-tenance, and devoid of grace. He is sorely neg-lected, poor man, for whilst his deacon, Marinus, stands proudly on the other side, adorned with flowers, and lighted by two handsome candles, his reverence is illumined by one solitary taper.

This statue of St. Marinus is strikingly different from all other Saints; his expression is full of conviviality, and his face is adorned with moustache and imperial, whilst in his hand he carries the heavy burden of three towers. It was removed from the parish church in the '*Città*' when the new one was put up, and is much more characteristic and expressive than the handsome work of art which has superseded it. In the corner of the church is seen a secluded hole in the wall; here a seat is set apart for the Captains, connected with the church by a small window; here they perform their devotions, when chance or residence may oblige them to pray in the provinces, and here their dazzling magnificence will not distract the attention of the admiring peasantry.

The noble families in this Republic are in a position peculiar to themselves; they never had any feudal character, but rose spontaneously from merit and inherent respect. These families, from amongst whom one of the Duumvirs must be selected, were only first distinguished as such towards the beginning of the seventeenth cen-

tury, when the Council recognised the necessity
of always having one Captain who was educated,
and could read and write, difficulties having
frequently arisen from two highly esteemed but
ignorant peasants being placed in so responsible
a position. Hence certain families were set
apart, from whom one of the Captains must be
selected to obviate this difficulty, and a sort of
nominal aristocracy arose; and on the extinction
of any of these families another is always elected
in its place, but in all other respects the equality
of rights enjoyed by all Sammarinesi is thus in
no way interfered with.

At the time when the French Revolution
shook Europe to its basis, the spirit of democracy
was felt even in this remote corner of the world;
and the Council of Sixty so far gave way to the
spirit of the times as to abolish the patriciate.
'And thus,' says Marino Fattori, 'this order,
established about the middle of the seventeenth
century to provide for the wants of the period,
bad in nought but name, fell without defending
itself in any way, and gave up a right, which
certainly had never been useful to itself, but

from which, at different times, the country had
derived much satisfaction, and simply because
the nobility of San Marino had always retained
its innocency; and in 1806, when Europe returned to its constitutional monarchies, it was
re-established, with the consent and will of those
very men who three years before had voluntarily
abolished it.'

San Marino, in common with other independent States, can confer titles on meritorious
individuals, but these are always given to foreigners who have in some way contributed to
the wellbeing of the State. Thus the Count
d'Avigdor, San Marino's representative at the
Courts of Paris and London, was made Duke
of Acquaviva, which title is recognised in the
'Paris Diplomatic Annual' of 1865. His widow
was, as has been mentioned, a great benefactress
to the State. Several others have received similar
recognition of services done for the Republic,
though they never confer any title, or the order
of knighthood, on any native of San Marino, for
fear of interfering with the recognised principles
of equality.

The honorary right of citizenship has frequently been conferred on persons who have resided in the Republic, or in any way brought honour to the State. Melchiore Delfico, the historian, was made a citizen; Count Borghese, the numismatist, who resided here for so many years; also Canova, who, in recognition of this honour, presented the Republic with a bronze bust of Napoleon, a copy of his own work in marble, which stands in the Council Chamber, with an inscription to testify the fact.

If anyone comes to reside at San Marino, it is necessary for him to have been six years with his family in the place before he can present a petition for naturalisation; then the Council, having taken into consideration his character during this time, and his fitness to become a Sammarinese, may elect him, and his family, to all the rights of citizenship, and not till then can he purchase land within the Republican precincts.

In the year 1859 an Equestrian Order was instituted, with which many illustrious foreigners are decorated. The purpose was expressed as follows, at the institution of the Order: 'The Council Sovereign of the Republic of San Marino, arrived at the fifteenth century from its foundation, and imbued with the most lively gratitude towards Divine Providence, towards

BADGE OF EQUESTRIAN ORDER.

S. Marino their founder, and towards all Sovereigns its perpetual and kindly protectors, and equally imbued with the necessity of showing their recognition towards those who have so effectively co-operated to the conservation and glory of the Republic, or to whom gratitude is

due from humanity, science, and art, has
decreed ' to institute this Order, &c. ; on the
register of which we find the names of Victor
Emmanuel, the Emperor of Germany, Napoleon
III. and his son, Prince Bismarck, and other
notable characters from various countries.

The right of conferring this Order is vested
solely in the hands of the Grand Council. The
Captains for the time being are Grand Masters
of this Order, to which they belong only during
their term of office, and are decorated with its
insignia at the time of their installation.

www.ingramcontent.com/pod-product-compliance
Lightning Source LLC
Chambersburg PA
CBHW030618030726
47497CB00006B/1550